SERVICE COMPUTATION 2018

The Tenth International Conferences on Advanced Service Computing

February 18 - 22, 2018

Barcelona, Spain

SERVICE COMPUTATION 2018 Editors

Arne Koschel, Hochschule Hannover, Germany

Janusz Klink, Wrocław University of Science and Technology, Wroclaw, Poland

Andreas Hausotter, Hochschule Hannover, Germany

Printed from e-media with permission by:

Curran Associates, Inc.
57 Morehouse Lane
Red Hook, NY 12571

Printed by Curran Associates, Inc. (2018)

International Academy, Research, and Industry Association (IARIA)
412 Derby Way
Wilmington, DE 19810

Phone: (408) 893-6407
Fax: (408) 527-6351

petre@iaria.org

Additional copies of this publication are available from:

Curran Associates, Inc.
57 Morehouse Lane
Red Hook, NY 12571 USA
Phone: 845-758-0400
Fax: 845-758-2633
Email: curran@proceedings.com
Web: www.proceedings.com

Table of Contents

SERVICE COMPUTATION 2018

Forward

The Tenth International Conferences on Advanced Service Computing (SERVICE COMPUTATION 2018), held between February 18 - 22, 2018 - Barcelona, Spain, continued a series of events targeting computation on different facets.

The ubiquity and pervasiveness of services, as well as their capability to be context-aware with (self-) adaptive capacities posse challenging tasks for services orchestration, integration, and integration. Some services might require energy optimization, some might require special QoS guarantee in a Web-environment, while others a certain level of trust. The advent of Web Services raised the issues of self-announcement, dynamic service composition, and third party recommenders. Society and business services rely more and more on a combination of ubiquitous and pervasive services under certain constraints and with particular environmental limitations that require dynamic computation of feasibility, deployment and exploitation.

The conference had the following tracks:

- Service innovation, evaluation and delivery
- Service quality
- Challenges
- Advanced Analysis of Service Compositions

Similar to the previous edition, this event attracted excellent contributions and active participation from all over the world. We were very pleased to receive top quality contributions.

We take here the opportunity to warmly thank all the members of the SERVICE COMPUTATION 2018 technical program committee, as well as the numerous reviewers. The creation of such a high quality conference program would not have been possible without their involvement. We also kindly thank all the authors that dedicated much of their time and effort to contribute to SERVICE COMPUTATION 2018. We truly believe that, thanks to all these efforts, the final conference program consisted of top quality contributions.

Also, this event could not have been a reality without the support of many individuals, organizations and sponsors. We also gratefully thank the members of the SERVICE COMPUTATION 2018 organizing committee for their help in handling the logistics and for their work that made this professional meeting a success.

We hope SERVICE COMPUTATION 2018 was a successful international forum for the exchange of ideas and results between academia and industry and to promote further progress in the area of computation. We also hope that Barcelona provided a pleasant environment during the conference and everyone saved some time for exploring this beautiful city.

SERVICE COMPUTATION 2018 Chairs

SERVICE COMPUTATION Steering Committee

Mihhail Matskin, KTH, Sweden
Bernhard Hollunder, Hochschule Furtwangen University – Furtwangen, Germany
Paul Humphreys, Ulster Business School/University of Ulster, UK
Arne Koschel, Hochschule Hannover, Germany
Michele Ruta, Technical University of Bari, Italy
Alfred Zimmermann, Reutlingen University, Germany
Aida Omerovic, SINTEF, Norway
Annett Laube, Bern University of Applied Sciences (BUAS), Switzerland
Claus Pahl, Dublin City University, Ireland

SERVICE COMPUTATION 2018 Industry/Research Advisory Committee

Marcelo De Barros, Microsoft, USA
Steffen Fries, Siemens Corporate Technology - Munich, Germany
Matthias Olzmann, noventum consulting GmbH - Münster, Germany
Rong N. Chang, IBM T.J. Watson Research Center, USA
Jan Porekar, SETCCE, Slovenia

SERVICE COMPUTATION 2018

Committee

Rong N. Chang, IBM T.J. Watson Research Center, USA
Dickson Chiu, The University of Hong Kong, Hong Kong
Marcelo De Barros, Microsoft, USA
Chiara Di Francescomarino, Fondazione Bruno Kessler (FBK), Italy
Leandro Dias da Silva, Instituto de Computação | Universidade Federal de Alagoas, Brazil
Chen (Cherie) Ding, Ryerson University, Canada
Erdogan Dogdu, TOBB University of Economics and Technology, Turkey
Cédric Eichler, LIFO-INSA Centre Val de Loire, France
José Enrique Armendáriz-Íñigo, Public University of Navarre, Spain
Sören Frey, Daimler TSS GmbH, Germany
Steffen Fries, Siemens Corporate Technology - Munich, Germany
Somchart Fugkeaw, University of Tokyo, Japan
Filippo Gaudenzi, Università Degli Studi di Milano, Italy
Verena Geist, Software Competence Center Hagenberg GmbH, Austria
Katja Gilly, Universidad Miguel Hernández, Spain
Victor Govindaswamy, Concordia University - Chicago, USA
Steven Guan (Sheng-Uei Guan), Jiaotong-Liverpool University, China
Tom Guérout, LAAS-CNRS | Université de Toulouse, France
Maki K. Habib, The American University in Cairo, Egypt
Andreas Hausotter, Hochschule Hannover - University of Applied Sciences and Arts, Germany
Martin Henkel, Stockholm University, Sweden
Bernhard Hollunder, Hochschule Furtwangen University – Furtwangen, Germany
Wladyslaw Homenda, Warsaw University of Technology, Poland
Tzung-Pei Hong, National University of Kaohsiung, Taiwan
Wei-Chiang Hong, Nanjing Tech University, China
Sun-Yuan Hsieh, National Cheng Kung University, Taiwan
Marc Hüffmeyer, Furtwangen University, Germany
Marc-Philippe Huget, Polytech Annecy-Chambery-LISTIC | University of Savoie, France
Paul Humphreys, Ulster University, UK
Hemant Jain, University of Tennessee at Chattanooga, USA
E. E. Jan, IBM Global Technology Services, USA
Maria João Ferreira, Universidade Portucalense, Portugal
Eleanna Kafeza, Athens University of Economics and Business, Greece
Yu Kaneko, Research and Development Center - Toshiba, Japan
Fu-Chien Kao, Da-Yeh University, Taiwan
Marouane Kessentini, University of Michigan - Dearborn, USA
Moahmmad Maifi Hasan Khan, University of Connecticut, USA
Peter Kilpatrick, Queen's University Belfast, UK
Hyunsung Kim, Kyungil University, Korea
Alexander Kipp, Robert Bosch GmbH, Germany
Janusz Klink, Wroclaw University of Science and Technology, Poland
Michal Kökörcený, Unicorn College / University of Hradec Králové, Czech Republic
Arne Koschel, Hochschule Hannover - University of Applied Sciences and Arts, Germany
Andrew Kusiak, The University of Iowa, USA
Annett Laube, Bern University of Applied Sciences (BUAS), Switzerland
Tian Lan, George Washington University, USA
Cho-Chin Lin, National Ilan University, Taiwan
Mark Little, Red Hat, UK

Qing Liu, Data61 - CSIRO, Australia
Xiaodong Liu, Edinburgh Napier University, UK
Luigi Lo Iacono, TH Köln, Germany
Francesco Longo, University of Messina, Italy
Shikharesh Majumdar, Carleton University, Canada
Kurt Maly, Old Dominion University, USA
Zoltan Mann, University of Duisburg-Essen, Germany
Mihhail Matskin, KTH, Sweden
Massimo Mecella, Sapienza Università di Roma, Italy
Viktor Medvedev, Vilnius University - Institute of Mathematics and Informatics, Lithuania
Michele Melchiori, DII - Università degli Studi di Brescia, Italy
Fanchao Meng, University of Delaware, USA
Philippe Merle, Inria Lille - Nord Europe, France
António Miguel Rosado da Cruz, Politechnic Institute of Viana do Castelo, Portugal
Naouel Moha, Université du Québec à Montréal, Canada
Mohamed Mohamed, IBM - Almaden Research Center, USA
Fernando Moreira, Universidade Portucalense, Portugal
Gero Muehl, Universitaet Rostock, Germany
Taiga Nakamura, IBM Research - Almaden Research Center, USA
Joan Navarro, La Salle - Universitat Ramon Llull, Spain
Artur Niewiadomski, Institute of Computer Science - Siedlce University of Natural Sciences and Humanities, Poland
Matthias Olzmann, noventum consulting, Germany
Aida Omerovic, SINTEF, Norway
Ali Ouni, Ecole de Technologie Superieure, Montreal, Canada
Claus Pahl, Dublin City University, Ireland
Paulo F. Pires, Federal University of Rio de Janeiro, Brazil
Agostino Poggi, DII - University of Parma, Italy
Jan Porekar, SETCCE, Slovenia
Pasqualina Potena, RISE SICS Västerås, Sweden
Thomas E. Potok, Oak Ridge National Laboratory, USA
Thomas M. Prinz, Friedrich Schiller University Jena, Germany
Lianyong Qi, Nanjing University, China
Neilson Ramalho, Wirecard Technologies GmbH, Munich, Germany
José Raúl Romero, University of Córdoba, Spain
Christoph Reich, Furtwangen University, Germany
Wolfgang Reisig, Humboldt University, Berlin, Germany
Feliz Ribeiro Gouveia, Fernando Pessoa University, Portugal
Sashko Ristov, University of Innsbruck, Austria
Juha Röning, University of Oulu, Finland
Michele Ruta, Technical University of Bari, Italy
Ulf Schreier, Furtwangen University, Germany
Frank Schulz, SAP Research Karlsruhe, Germany
Wael Sellami, Higher Institute of Computer Sciences of Mahdia, Tunisia
Kuei-Ping Shih, Tamkang University, Taiwan
Jacopo Soldani, University of Pisa, Italy
Masakazu Soshi, Hiroshima City University, Japan
George Spanoudakis, City University of London, UK

Abhishek Srivastava, Indian Institute of Technology Indore, India
Young-Joo Suh, POSTECH, Korea
Orazio Tomarchio, Universita' di Catania, Italy
Alberto Trombetta, University of Insubria, Italy
David Wallom, Oxford e-Research Centre | University of Oxford, UK
Yong Wang, Dakota State University, USA
Hironori Washizaki, Waseda University, Japan
Mandy Weißbach, Martin-Luther-University Halle-Wittenberg, Germany
Jian Yu, Auckland University of Technology, New Zealand
Michael Zapf, Georg Simon Ohm University of Applied Sciences, Germany
Sherali Zeadally, University of Kentucky, USA
Wenbing Zhao, Cleveland State University, USA
Alfred Zimmermann, Reutlingen University, Germany
Wolf Zimmermann, Martin Luther University Halle-Wittenberg, Germany
Christian Zirpins, Karlsruhe University of Applied Sciences, Germany
Albert Zomaya, University of Sydney, Australia

Copyright Information

Using Service-oriented Architectures for Online Surveys in *Coast*

Thomas M. Prinz, Raphael Bernhardt, Linda Gräfe, Jan Plötner, and Anja Vetterlein
Course Evaluation Service
Friedrich Schiller University Jena
Jena, Germany
e-mail: {Thomas.Prinz, Raphael.Bernhardt, Linda.Graefe, Jan.Ploetner, Anja.Vetterlein}@uni-jena.de

***Abstract*—Electronic surveys are used in empirical sciences in many cases to reach a large and global crowd. Such surveys can be separated into five big phases (e. g., planning and data collection), where each phase belongs to each other. Since the interdependencies between the phases are sometimes complex, it is helpful to have a software system, which supports each phase of a survey. There already exist such systems, which cover together all of the phases. However, the focus is on the implementation of the survey rather than on its evaluation and reporting. This was one reason to build a new survey and report tool, *Coast*. The first version of *Coast*, however, has some disadvantages regarding its monolithic architecture — a new version of *Coast* had to be developed. This paper presents the new version of *Coast* as a practical result and example of service-oriented systems. The architecture of *Coast* is built on concepts of service orientation and model-driven software development. Furthermore, the paper explains the big design decisions during development, describes parts of the used meta-models, and shows some practical problems during the development of service-oriented programs and how they are solved in *Coast*.**

Keywords–Service Orientation; Architecture; Coast; Survey; Model-Driven Software Development.

I. INTRODUCTION

Surveys are indispensable in empirical sciences (for example in psychology and sociology). In many cases, it is profitable to use an *electronic* or *online* survey to reach a large and locally dispersed crowd (e. g., [1]). An electronic survey can be separated in different phases, e. g., survey implementation, data collection, and reporting [2]. Each of the phases is interwoven with the other. For example, the reporting phase needs the specific questions asked in the survey as well as the different variables and scales from the implementation phase. In turn, the collected data can only be interpreted by knowing the scales and variables they belong to. So, it is very helpful to have a software system, which supports each of the phases of a survey.

Such software tools are available on the market, e. g., *EvaSys* [3], *Unipark* [4], *LimeSurvey* [5], *KwikSurveys* [6], and *SurveyMonkey* [7]. Most of them cover parts of all phases of a survey. Almost all tools provide only a predefined or simple evaluation and reporting, since the evaluation and reporting phase are very individual processes and can become quite complex. For further analyses (e. g., multivariate analyses) exceeding the standard repertoire, these tools offer the download of the raw data instead. This, however, disrupts the link between the data and the other phases of a survey — the individual evaluation becomes a time consuming and cumbersome task even when the link to the other phases can be simulated with further provided information.

This fact was one of the main reasons of the *Course Evaluation Center* at the Friedrich Schiller University Jena in the year 2009 to build its own survey and report tool, called *Coast*. It focuses on the integration of the analysis and report phases for advanced analyses. Although it is in successful use for the evaluation of the university, the first version of *Coast* has its disadvantages. The disadvantages resulted from varying requirements, wrong design decisions, and surveys, which getting complexer as the architecture can handle. A monolithic architecture emerged [8], which makes it hard and risky to implement changes on the business logic.

As a result, a new version of the *Coast* application is currently under development. This new version removes the disadvantages from the first version by clarifying the architecture and modules as well as the model of *questionnaires* and reports. In this context, a *questionnaire* refers to all the questions, scales, etc. being necessary to collect the data.

In this short paper, we present parts of our tool *Coast* as an example of a service-oriented software. Furthermore, we give a brief overview about the phases of an electronic survey and already existing survey solutions in Section II. In Section III, we show the architecture of our system as a practical example and explain some design decisions as well as the meta-model of questionnaires used by *Coast*. Eventually, we conclude this paper with a short outlook into future work in Section IV.

II. STATE OF THE ART

In the following, we explain the five big phases of an electronic survey and give a brief overview about existing solutions for creating and carrying out online surveys.

A. Phases of an Electronic Survey

A survey can be separated into five big phases [2]:

1) Planning, design, and implementation,
2) Data collection,
3) Data preparation,
4) Data analysis, and
5) Reporting.

The first phase, *Planning, design, and implementation*, includes *planning* on what you want to ask, *deciding* how to ask these questions and how to measure concepts of interest, and *specifying* who will be surveyed (the *population*). Furthermore, the survey will be implemented. That implementation is used in the second phase to survey the population. This phase is called *Data collection*. Since the collected data may comprise malformed, incomplete, or obviously wrong records, the data has to be cleaned and prepared (*Data preparation* phase) to be used in a *Data analysis*, the fourth phase, afterwards. In this phase, the collected data is analysed in order to answer the questions from the first phase. The results of the evaluation as well as general information about the survey are finally summarized in detail in a report. The report is the outcome of the last phase, *Reporting*.

B. Other Survey Tools

Obviously, *Coast* is not the only survey tool available on the market supporting the phases of a survey. There are well-established tools with a lot of features like *EvaSys* [3], *Unipark* [4], *LimeSurvey* [5], *KwikSurveys* [6], and *SurveyMonkey* [7]. All of them cover parts of the previously introduced five phases of an electronic survey. They provide an implementation of the questionnaire by simply drag and drop the survey questions on a paper-like sheet in almost all products. The resulting questionnaire can be used for the data collection subsequently. In the case of *EvaSys*, it is possible to produce paper-based questionnaires too and scan them to collect the results.

The phases of data preparation, data analysis, and reporting are not clearly separated in most of the tools and, therefore, merge smoothly. All the tools have the possibility to export the collected data for further investigations in external tools (e.g., *IBM SPSS* [9], *Excel* [10], or *R* [11]). Furthermore, they provide standardized reports, which include the questions of the questionnaires, frequencies, significance tests, and mean values, among other things.

III. The System Architecture of *Coast*

The tools mentioned above show a clear focus on the development of the survey instead of its fine-granular and complex data analysis and reporting. As mentioned before, this was one reason to build an own survey tool *Coast*.

The first version of *Coast* had a monolithic software architecture caused by historical growing and changing requirements. Therefore, it showed the typical symptoms of monolithic software systems, e. g., changes on the business logic were difficult and risked the instability of the system. It is well-known that such architectures are some of the "worst" forms of architectures established in practice [8].

As the questionnaires handled by *Coast* became more complex, the usage of the first *Coast* version was not longer possible. However, the tools introduced in Section II-B cannot handle our complex questionnaires without bigger changes on the questionnaire structure (and questions asked in the survey). Since we use longitudinal analyses [12] (which require equal questionnaires during each data collection), it is necessary to keep the existing structure intact. Therefore, it is *not* possible to use a different survey tool. This makes it necessary to transfer our tool *Coast* into a different architecture. We explain our decisions for the main architectural approaches in the following:

As mentioned in Section II-A, making an electronic survey is an almost well-defined process. The same holds true with the modelling of questionnaires. It is our goal for *Coast* to offer a proper, controlled, and realistic modelling and development of questionnaires, i. e., we want to provide a *domain-specific language* (DSL) to model questionnaires. As a result of this approach, the focus lies on the *meta-model* of a questionnaire, whose instance is in turn the result of the modelling. The focus on the meta-model of questionnaires makes it possible to derive different kinds of surveys from the same model: For example, surveys represented online on PC, on paper, or on smart phones. Therefore, we follow a *Model driven software development* (MDSD) approach [8].

By using a MDSD architecture, the models are transferred into, e. g., runnable surveys, by using different functions. Since these functions could be long running and computational expensive tasks, they should not affect, e. g., the data collection of a survey. That means, the functions should *scale* and be physical *separable*. With *Service-oriented architectures* (SOA) [8] such a separation and scalability is easy and, therefore, a good choice.

In general, *Coast* is a typical enterprise application consisting of a client-side, a database, and a server-side. Its architecture is built around the meta-model for questionnaires and reports (as illustrated in Figure 1). Furthermore, the architecture can be separated into the five phases of a survey (cf. Section II-A). Subsequently, the phase architecture of Figure 1 will be explained.

The phase of planning, designing and implementing surveys is solved with a *Survey designer* on the client-side. It is a web tool, which communicates via services to transmit changes on the model of the client- to the server-side. *Designer services* help to commit these changes from the designer to the model.

As mentioned before, different implementations of surveys can be derived originating from the *questionnaire model* via different *Survey generator services*. For example, this could be *paper-based surveys* or *online surveys*. These generated surveys can be used to collect the data subsequently. For the online surveys, there is also a *database*, in which the collected data is stored.

Besides different derivable surveys, the *report model* can be derived from the questionnaire model as well. This is done by a *Transformation service*. It transforms the questionnaire structures and transfers the texts (e. g., formulations of questions) to a new report model. Furthermore, the collected data from the surveys are verified based on the questionnaire model by *Preparation services*. During this verification process, malformed and incorrect data is identified. Therefore, the preparation services belongs to the data preparation phase.

The verified and collected data is used for the data analysis. The data is analysed with the functionality of the statistical programming language *R* via *Analysis and report services*. Therefore, complex calculations, like tests of significance, filters, or regressions, can be applied on the data. To structure the report and use the evaluated data, an *Analysis and report designer* is available. Since the report exists as model, it can be also transformed to different kinds of "physical" reports, e. g., *online* or *paper-based reports*. This is done by the use of different *Report generator services*

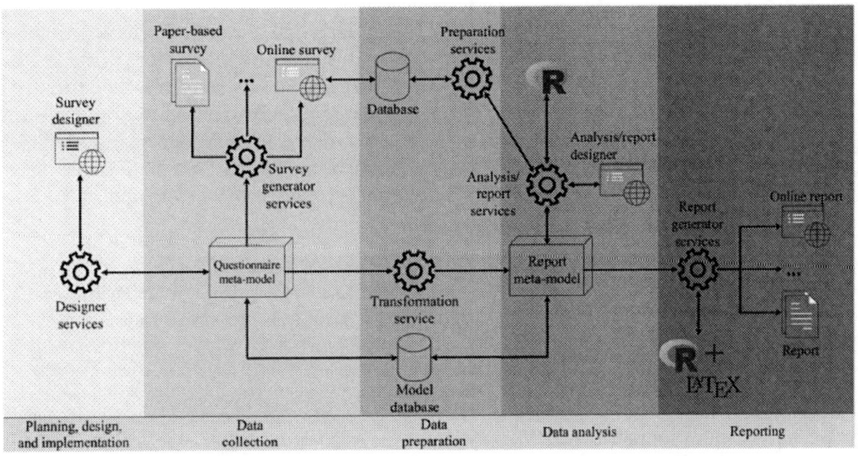

Figure 1. The architecture of the *Coast* system regarding the survey phases.

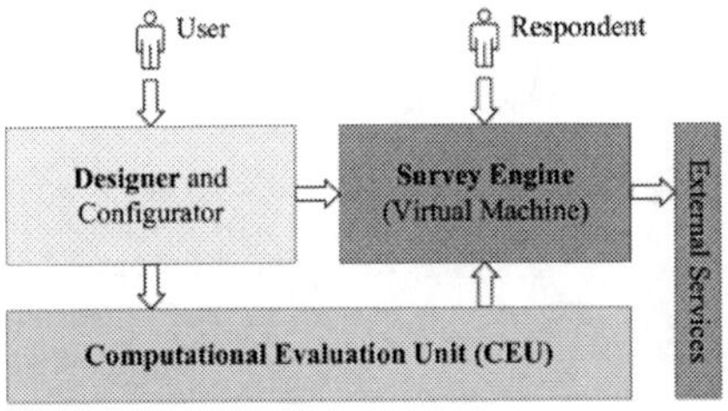

Figure 2. The component architecture of the *Coast* system.

and the inclusion of *R* and *LaTeX*.

Since the important parts of the architecture follow ongoing research in the context of psychoinformatics and compiler construction, they have to be flexible, simple, and evolutionarily growable. These requirements are complied by the use of the principles of service orientation and *microservices* [13]. Using (micro)services requires the *componentization* of the application into subsystems and modules (services).

In general, *Coast* disintegrates into three bigger subsystems: *Designer and Configurator* (in the following simply referred to *Designer*), *Survey Engine*, and *Computational Evaluation Unit* (CEU, illustrated in Figure 2). The *Designer* is the main application, in which the surveys will be defined, evaluated, and bundled in a report. In the *Survey Engine*, the surveys are conducted and the collected data is stored. The last subsystem CEU performs calculations for the analysis.

Each module of *Coast* is defined as a service with its own interface. If the functionality of the service is shared with other subsystems or a user, it will be provided as a *RESTful* web interface. Otherwise, it is a simple programming interface for reasons of performance. The arrows in Figure 2 explain how the subsystems interact with each other.

The *CEU* does not have a user interface as shown in the figure. It is a fully *computational* service only used for statistical calculations. It is based on the scripting language *R*, which is perfect for analysing big data information and to apply multivariate analysis methods. A *Coast* specific *R* library is supplied by an *openCPU* [14] server as a RESTful web service.

In contrast to the *CEU*, the subsystems *Designer* as well as the *Survey Engine* have a user interface. In the *Designer*, the user configures its surveys and transfers them to the *Survey Engine* where a participant can fill in the questionnaires — together, both subsystems follow an old computer science principle: Compilation and execution. Since the engine is separated from the designer, it is possible to have multiple *Survey Engine* service instances on different physical systems. As a result, the survey conduct becomes scalable. For this, the compiler (*Designer*) stores the survey in an intermediate representation (*IR*) called *liQuid* [15] and, afterwards, this IR will be transferred to the *Survey Engine*, which executes it. To guarantee equal data structures on both subsystem, they share the same modules.

It has become best practice during the *Coast* development to maintain each module (not only the subsystems) as a separate project and to build up the subsystems based on them. This approach helped us to generalize modules, to define proper interfaces, to get loosely coupled functionality, and to reuse code whenever possible.

For example, one module defines our meta-model for questionnaires. It is natural to think about questionnaires as sheets of paper with well-formulated questions. However, electronic surveys offer more ways to think of questionnaires than it is traditionally done in state-of-the-art tools. Instead, *Coast* treats questionnaires as program-like constructs. That means, in *Coast*, questionnaires have a well-defined start point, they have questions (*items*), whose order can be defined by acyclic graphs, and the order of these items depends on different conditions. In other words, questionnaires are acyclic *control flow graphs*.

Figure 3 shows the simplified meta-model of questionnaires used in *Coast*. It consists of the *questionnaire* with *edges* and *items*. Each edge has one item as *source* and one

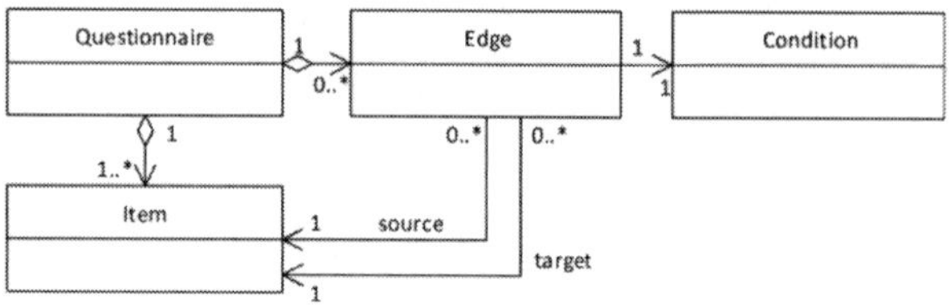

Figure 3. The meta-model of a questionnaire.

as *target* as well as a condition, which defines when this edge should be followed during the data collection.

First benefits of using such a control flow graph-based meta model of questionnaires were shown in previous work [15]. For example, we have a questionnaire, which is used to survey alumni of the university. Since all alumni have an individual career, the questionnaire became very complex with many so-called *adaptive* paths and variables. The visualization of the questionnaire model as a graph helped us to keep the overview of all paths and variables as well as to maintain the central theme. Furthermore, it is possible, to apply the complete palette of static and dynamic analyses of compiler construction, e. g., asking the same item multiple times on the same path.

The fine-grained meta-models for the definition of questionnaires and reports result in big models of sometimes hundreds to thousands objects. If a user wants to modify such a model within its web application, all those objects have to be taken from the database and have to be sent to the client. Sometimes, this took more than 30 seconds — which is unacceptable. Therefore, the pattern of *lazy loading* [16] objects was used. This was done by replacing each association of objects with a symbolic link, e. g., with an id and the corresponding object class. When the client application tries to access an associated object, the system loads the required object from the server automatically if it was not already loaded before. Nevertheless, to allow a straight forward modelling and programming, the concept of promises [17] was extended to an ordinary if-then-construct making the programming of asynchronous applications easy.

Certainly, there are some issues on *Coast* and its architecture. For example, sometimes, the performance of the system is slower than in the first monolithic application. This comes from the increased overhead by using a service-oriented architecture. Furthermore, there are sometimes a lot of messages being transferred between the different services. Especially, the communication between the client and the server during the design of a questionnaire is verbose. Although there are these weaknesses on the current design, the chosen one has shown its benefits so far.

IV. Conclusion and Outlook

This short paper explained the benefits of having a software in empirical sciences, which allows the control of all survey phases. As an example of such a tool, we introduced our tool *Coast*, which focuses on the analysis and report phases of a survey. Using the example of *Coast*, we explained our design decisions, why we used a model-driven software and a service-oriented architecture. Furthermore, parts of its architecture were presented as practical examples.

Since the *Coast* system is currently in an alpha version, *Coast* is unpublished up to now. In future versions, it should be available to everyone via the web. For this purpose, the application has to reach a stable stage and some of the concepts have to be extended.

References

[1] V. M. Sue and L. A. Ritter, Conducting Online Surveys, 2nd ed. Los Angeles, USA: SAGE Publications, 2012.

[2] J. Reinecke, Handbuch Methoden der empirischen Sozialforschung. Wiesbaden, Germany: Springer, 2014, vol. 1, ch. Grundlagen der standardisierten Befragung, pp. 601–617.

[3] Electric Paper Ltd., "Survey Automation Software - EvaSys and EvaExam," Website, available: http://en.evasys.de/main/home.html, retrieved: January, 2018.

[4] QuestBack GmbH, "Startseite — Unipark," Website, available: https://www.unipark.com/en/, retrieved: January, 2018.

[5] LimeSurvey GmbH, "LimeSurvey: the online survey tool - open source surveys," Website, available: https://www.limesurvey.org/, retrieved: January, 2018.

[6] Problem Free Ltd., "KwikSurveys: Free online survey & questionnaire tool," Website, available: https://kwiksurveys.com/, retrieved: January, 2018.

[7] SurveyMonkey, "SurveyMonkey: The Worlds Most Popular Free Online Survey Tool," Website, available: https://www.surveymonkey.com/, retrieved: January, 2018.

[8] O. Vogel, I. Arnold, A. Chughtai, E. Ihler, T. Kehrer, U. Mehlig, and U. Zdun, Software-Architektur: Grundlagen - Konzepte - Praxis, 2nd ed. Heidelberg, Germany: Springer, 2009.

[9] IBM United Kingdom Limited, "IBM SPSS Statistics - Overview - United Kingdom," Website, available: https://www.ibm.com/uk-en/marketplace/spss-statistics, retrieved: January, 2018.

[10] Microsoft, "Microsoft Excel 2016, Download Spreadsheet software — XLS XLSX," Website, available: https://products.office.com/en-gb/excel, retrieved: January, 2018.

[11] The R Foundation, "R: The R Project for Statistical Computing," Website, available: https://www.r-project.org/, retrieved: January, 2018.

[12] T. Mika and M. Stegmann, Handbuch Methoden der empirischen Sozialforschung. Wiesbaden, Germany: Springer, 2014, vol. 1, ch. Längsschnittanalyse, pp. 1077–1087.

[13] J. Lewis and M. Fowler, "Microservices — A definition of this new architectural term," matinfowler.com, Online publication, Mar. 2014, available: https://martinfowler.com/articles/microservices.html#footnote-etymology, retrieved: January, 2018.

[14] J. Ooms, "The OpenCPU System: Towards a Universal Interface for Scientific Computing through Separation of Concerns," Computing Research Repository (CoRR), vol. abs/1406.4806, 2014, pp. 1–23.

[15] T. M. Prinz, L. Gräfe, J. Plötner, and A. Vetterlein, "Statische Aanalysen von Online-Befragungen mit der Programmiersprache *liQuid* (Static Aanalysis of Online Surveys with the Help of the Programming Language *liQuid*)," in Proceedings 19. Kolloquium Programmiersprachen und Grundlagen der Programmierung, KPS 2017, Weimar, Germany, pp. 59–70, September 25–27, 2017.

[16] M. Fowler, D. Rice, M. Foemmel, E. Hieatt, R. Mee, and R. Stafford, Patterns of Enterprise Application Architecture, 1st ed., M. Fowler, Ed. Boston, USA: Addison Wesley, 2003.

[17] B. Cavalier and D. Denicola, Promises/A+ Promise Specification, Open Access, Promises/A+ organization Std. 1.1.1, 2014, available: https://promisesaplus.com/, retrieved: January, 2018.

Incorporating Virtuality in Ubiquitous Computing Services for Influencing Human Behavior

Tatsuo Nakajima
Department of Computer Science and Engineering
Waseda University
Tokyo Japan
e-mail: tatsuo@dcl.cs.waseda.ac.jp

Kota Gushima
Department of Computer Science and Engineering
Waseda University
Tokyo Japan
e-mail: gushi@dcl.cs.waseda.ac.jp

Abstract—**The role of computing technologies has been expanding, and our lifestyles will be significantly influenced by these technologies. Refining the meaning of real space by incorporating virtuality through ubiquitous computing technologies is a very powerful concept because people's senses are enhanced, making them potentially see something that may not exist in the real space. For example, human eyesight can be altered using head-mounted displays, which modify real-world views captured by video cameras with mixed reality technologies. These approaches are also useful in influencing human behaviors that make a variety of new types of digital services possible. The paper presents four case studies to enhance the meaning of the real space through incorporating virtuality and proposes a design guideline extracted from the experience with their development.**

Keywords-Ubiquitous Computing; Mixed Reality; Virtual Reality; Augmented Reality; Virtuality; Head-Mounted Display;

I. INTRODUCTION

Ubiquitous computing technologies allow us to refine the meaning of our real space through incorporating virtuality for influencing our behaviors [12][20][25]. For example, recent advanced technologies, such as a Magic Leap's technology [9] and Microsoft HoloLens [10], can easily refine the meaning of our real space and offer new possibilities to change our daily lifestyle. For example, human eyesight can be altered using head-mounted displays (HMDs), which modify real-world views captured by video cameras with mixed reality technologies. For our daily life to become more sustainable and well-being, behavior changes are essential [12][24]. To alter our behaviors, the meaning of the real space must be refined through incorporating virtuality to make people believe that their changes have meaningful effects on our future and environments. However, there are very few researches on design strategies to refine the meaning of the real space through incorporating virtuality because such researches must take into account multiple different disciplines that are typically distinguished, and substantial effort is required to integrate them. For example, significant movie and animation content exploits virtuality to influence our daily behaviors; however, the discussions about design content would rather be isolated from the technology design of digital services, although ubiquitous computing technologies are essentially virtualizing our daily lives [3]. Therefore, although technology has sufficiently advanced, it is difficult to discuss how to guide the design of the refined real space valuably and meaningfully.

In this paper, our focus is to investigate a design guideline to examine the quality of virtuality. Existing researches have shown some design guidelines for developing augmented reality and virtual reality services. However, their focuses are to offer design guidelines to develop augmented reality services or to examine the quality of virtuality in virtual spaces, and there are no good metrics to extract potential pitfalls of the quality of virtuality incorporated in real spaces. For extracting the guideline, we first present four case studies to enhance the meaning of the real space through incorporating virtuality. By incorporating virtuality that does not exist in the real space that we currently see, our behaviors can be influenced then altered [8][13][19][20][22][24][25]. The aims to develop these case studies have exploited to incorporate virtuality in our daily real life, and these case studies incorporate virtuality from diverse angles. Thus, they are appropriate to extract a guideline for designing virtuality embedded in real spaces. We then present a guideline extracted from the experience with their developments. Because the guideline focuses on the design of incorporated virtuality in real spaces, and finds potential pitfalls of the design; thus, it can complement other existing guidelines.

This paper is organized as follows. Section II presents some related work on this study. In Section III, we describe four case studies, and show a design guideline extracted from the experiences with building the case studies in Section IV. Finally, Section V concludes the paper.

II. RELATED WORK

Several existing services examine the use of augmented reality technologies to enhance the meaning of real space to influence people's attitudes and behaviors. For example, in [5], the authors reported on the concept of *Blended Virtuality*, whereby people use HMDs while downhill skiing and snowboarding. The user experiences a visually enhanced real space through the HMD without losing the full sensation of real-world skiing. In [13], the authors propose a service that using augmented reality technologies to implicitly influence the satisfaction that people experience when drinking a beverage and to control beverage consumption by creating a volume perception illusion. The system proposed in [22] aims to use augmented reality technologies as a way of modifying perceptions of satiety to control nutritional intake by changing the apparent size of food. In [25], several case studies to offer playful augmented reality applications that seamlessly integrate virtuality in real space are reported.

There are several researches to propose guidelines to develop services incorporating virtuality. For example, in [16], the authors present a guideline for the development process of mobile augmented reality applications. Also, in [23], some useful guidelines to develop better augmented reality games are described. In [25], the authors present guidelines to make traditional games more enjoyable by incorporating virtuality. These guidelines focus on how to develop services and applications to incorporate virtuarity in them, and they do not focus on the effective ways to design the quality of virtuality. Some other frameworks are also useful to help the design of virtuality from different angles. For example, the framework described in [18] shows some properties for designing meaningful virtuality. Also, in [20], the framework to categorize the type of virtuality is proposed.

However, currently, there are no sufficient discussions how to maintain the quality of incorporated virtuality in the real space. Although the approach is promising, but there is no proper design guidelines for designing virtuality used in real spaces in terms of the quality. The quality of virtuality is essential because a user does not want to use services that he/she feels a sense of incongruity in the incorporated virtuality in real spaces.

III. FOUR CASE STUDIES

A. *HoloMoL: Human Memory Augmentation with Mixed-Reality Technologies*

HoloLens, Microsoft's HMD, has recently attracted people to develop new services in a variety of fields. Microsoft HoloLens [10] is able to deliver a mixed reality user experience [1], allowing people to interact with virtual objects and entities within real world settings. Mixed reality technologies enable designers to develop new types of advanced services that incorporating virtuality into the real world. The software platform that accompanies the Microsoft HoloLens hardware enabled developing mixed reality applications easily without requiring advanced skills. Various visions of possible novel services have already been presented. We would like to investigate supporting memorization techniques as a new application domain for Microsoft HoloLens, where we adopt the method of loci which is an ancient Greek method that can be used to memorize different types of information [26]. The first case study is named *HoloMoL* (HoloLens's Method of Loci).

The main objective of *HoloMoL* is to support the method of loci for augmenting human memory with mixed reality technologies based on Microsoft HoloLens and to enable utilizing the method of loci with minimal training. The original method of loci enables people to memorize information by imagining a space in their mind and placing information in the such space. *HoloMoL* replaces the imaginary space with real world places that people also know well. *HoloMoL* automatically lays out information, that people intend to memorize, as AR entities within a real space. Thus, they experience the method of loci by moving in the real space, where corresponding information is automatically displayed using *HoloMoL*, so they are able to memorize the information as they navigate through the space.

Figure 1. A user places a fiducial marker in his preferred location in a real space for memorizing information

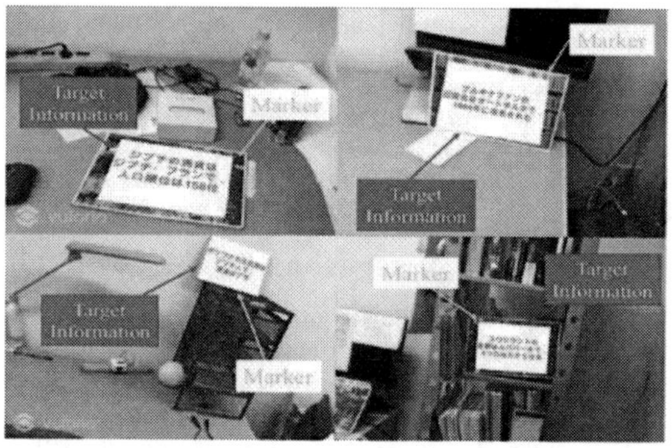

Figure 2. A user places respective fiducial makers that correspond to information to be memorized in difference places

HoloMoL provide the ability to display the corresponding information using mixed reality technologies when a person gazes at a specific position in a real space. When a person wears a Microsoft HoloLens device, the surroundings that are normally visible are the same as the actual view, but when he/she moves to a position specified by him/her in advance and recognizes a specific marker, the corresponding information is automatically displayed.

Our implementation utilizes fiducial markers to lay out various information registered to the real space as shown in Figures 1 and 2. Since *MoloMoL*'s objective is to investigate how people would place information for memorization, we decided to use printed fiducial markers that people were able to physically move and place around the environment. By placing a marker near any objects located in a real space, *HoloMoL* exploits associative memory to memorize a variety of information.

The current version of *HoloMoL* is developed as an application of Microsoft HoloLens. Unity is used as a software platform to render 3D contents in the real space, and Vuforia is adopted to recognize fiducial markers. The database implemented in *HoloMoL* associates the image of each marker to be recognized with the corresponding information to be displayed in the real space. When a marker is recognized, the database is referenced, and the corresponding information is displayed as a sequence of characters written on a plate-shaped object as shown in Figure 2.

B. *AmbientBot: Delivering Daily Casual Information through Eye Contact with an Intimate Virtual Creature*

Our daily life becomes increasingly rich through the progress of advanced digital technologies. In particular, our modern daily lifestyle has been dramatically changed because of smart phones that always connect us to the Internet, thus enabling access to various information sources anytime and anywhere. However, the current progress of information technologies significantly increases our cognitive overload. In our daily commute in Tokyo, for example, a tremendous amount of information is presented to us through public displays located in trains and stations. As shown in [15], various modern social media try to steal our available attention by using ubiquitous computing technologies. For making our daily life more comfortable and peaceful, information should be more ambiently and intimately delivered to us only when the information is really necessary. In addition, the information should be available to us without extra time and effort.

Figure 3. Ambient Bot Concept

The second case study, called *Ambient Bot*, presents an intimate virtual creature in the real space with augmented reality technologies. *Ambient Bot* arranges a virtual creature in a user' view as shown in Figure 3, but the creature leaves the user's scope when he/she does not want to receive any information from the creature. If some information wants to be received when becoming free, he/she tries to find the virtual creature in his/her current view.

When focusing his/her attention on the creature, it speaks and visualizes information to him/her, but when turning his/her attention away from the creature, it stops speaking. Therefore, the creature always but ambiently exists in the user's view, but does not disturb his/her current activities when not focusing his/her attention on the creature. *Ambient Bot* offers information in a social manner because the user feels an intimate relationship with the creature [17]; thus, the interaction with the creature will make his/her daily life richer [18], unlike traditional notification technologies that focus on only the efficiency through functionalism that sometimes offers tasteless interaction. Especially, for Japanese young adults who are very familiar with various anime and video game products, using intimate virtual creatures not highly functional inorganic products makes them feel more social and intimate relationship with advanced information technologies.

Ambient Bot shown in Figure 4 currently displays a jellyfish as a virtual creature in a user's surrounding space with augmented reality technologies, and the jellyfish speaks to the user when he makes eye contact with the jellyfish. He uses the prototype system by wearing an HMD; Oculus Rift is currently chosen as the HMD for *Ambient Bot*. As described in the previous section, we chose the latest news articles, weather forecast, or latest posts or trending words in a social media service were chosen as the content that the jellyfish speaks. In Figure 4, the left photo shows a user who wears an HMD for using Ambient Bot, and the center photo is a view that he actually sees the view through the HMD. When he makes eye contact with the jellyfish, the jellyfish turns to him, then speaks and presents appropriate contents to him. The content is retrieved from the Google News API, the LINE's WeatherHacks API, and the Twitter API. The content is converted into voice data through the Hoya's VoiceText Web API for the jellyfish to speak. The content is also shown on a user's HMD in real time when the jellyfish speaks the content.

C. *Augmented Bike: Building a Platform Society towards Sustainability*

This section presents the third case study named *Augmented Bike* for designing a social platform towards environmental sustainability based on Internet-of-Things. The case study we investigate encourages low carbon communities [6][7], in particular, to aim for a car-free city. A car-free city promises to make our society more sustainable [4]; however, people must be guided to choose a desirable lifestyle. *Augmented Bike* is an Internet of Things (IoT)-enhanced bicycle for promoting bicycle-sharing within communities. Bicycle sharing can help to achieve a car-free city, and IoT-based daily artifacts can contribute to building an effective social platform.

Augmented Bike is a digitally enhanced daily artifact that augments rental bicycles using VR and AR technologies. When a new wearable device such as Google Glass becomes popular and most people wear the device in the near future, the devices can be used for facilitating a car-free city by augmenting rental bicycles with the new wearable devices and motivating people to use a rental bicycle. Using an *Augmented Bike*, people can easily rent a bike by touching their IC cards or using a fingerprint or an implanted IC chip that contains their personal information. Let us imagine a situation in which people always use an HMD and the display does not impede their sight, unlike a current HMD such as Oculus Lift. *Augmented Bike* as

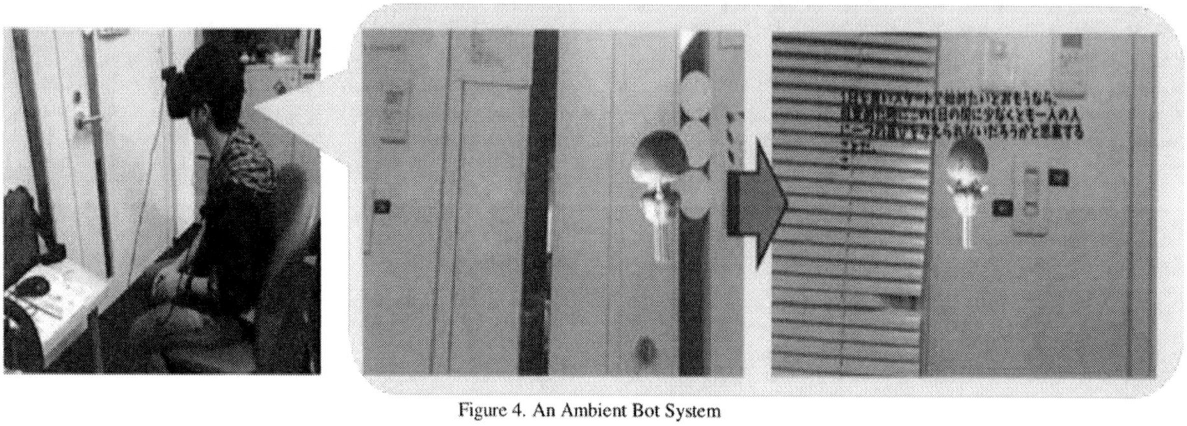

Figure 4. An Ambient Bot System

shown in Figure 5 enhances people's view and shows additional information on the HMDs that they wear. In addition, traveling distance and trail information are recorded on their smartphones, and people can check the information anytime. Figure 5 presents an overview of the *Augmented Bike* prototype.

When using the *Augmented Bike*, an application program displays the images that enhance a user's current real view on an HMD and shows pop-up information regarding the images to provide the rider with additional information. We also developed an application program that records traveling distance and trail information, and we offer some gamification effects using graphical changes.

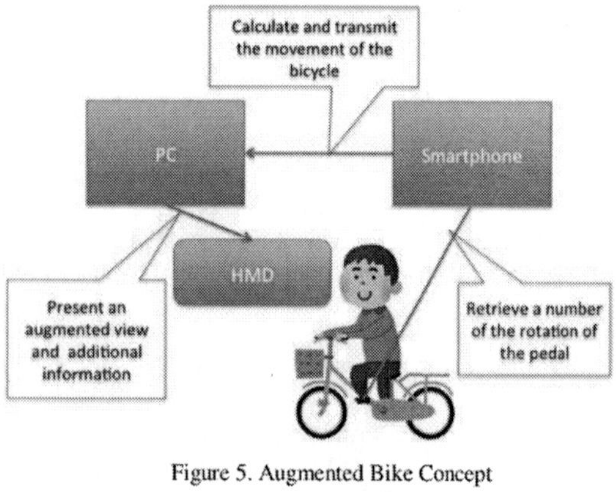

Figure 5. Augmented Bike Concept

The current *Augmented Bike* shown in Figure 6 uses Oculus Rift as an HMD. In a typical case, the video that is captured from the real world by a camera attached to Oculus Rift is shown to a user so that the user can use his eyes to see his surroundings and simultaneously see virtual scenes generated by virtual reality technology. The current prototype identifies a user by fingerprints taken before and after using the *Augmented Bike*. In addition, a smartphone application runs on Android OS, and we use Unity as a platform to execute our applications both for Oculus Lift and the smartphone. The programs are written in C# and use Node.js to communicate between two application programs. The smartphone application monitors the movement of the pedals of the *Augmented Bike* using an acceleration sensor and transmits the information to a PC. The program running on the PC generates images to Oculus Lift. Our current prototype must use a desktop PC now although the prototype will work on a more powerful smartphone in the near future.

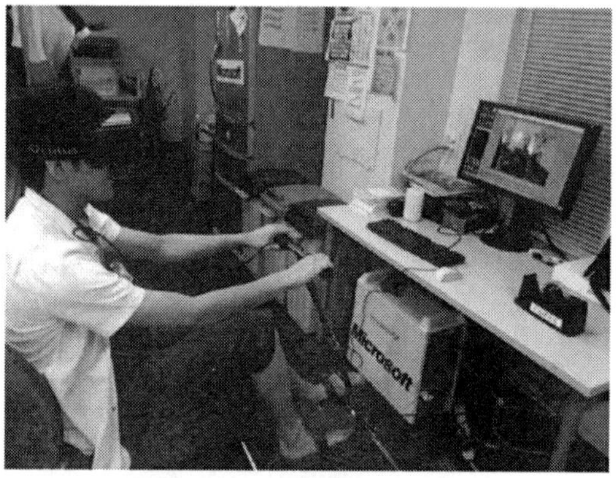

Figure 6. An Experiment Using the Augmented Bike

D. Mindful Reminder: Increasing a User's Empathy toward His/Her Surrounding Environment

At present, various useful digital services already enrich people's daily lives. For example, sharing economy services and social networking services have become popular. These services allow us communicate with other people in a new and different way, making human relationships more meaningful. These relationships make us more mindful of various aspects of our daily lives because these services exploit new opportunities to enhance serendipitous human relationships. However, our modern daily lives increasingly busy, and we sometimes forget to empathize with other people, even though emerging digital services facilitate human relationships. In particular, information technologies provide various notifications to keep the user mindful and calm, thereby reducing the overextension of human cognitive resources and using those resources more effectively [2]. However, current notification technologies exploit peripheral attention and make our daily lives inorganic because such notifications do not facilitate human relationships.

Thus, the effect of these notification services is not strong enough to make people's lives really flourish. Of course, many digital services already notify us about important issues in our daily lives; for example, a calendar service notifies a person about his/her schedule, and a reminder service tells him/her what he/she needs to do. However, the information is typically sent through smartphones or laptops; thus, although the services increase the richness of our daily lives in terms of efficiency, we flourish less in our daily lives and forget about people's feelings and empathy, which is important to make our daily lives mindful and calm when the number of notifications increases.

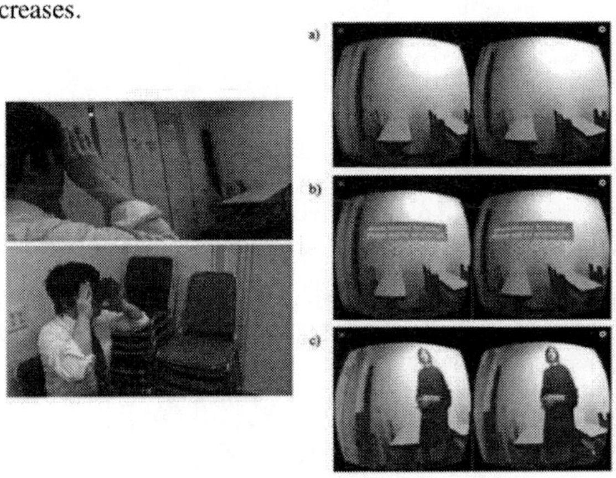

Figure 7. An Overview of Mindful Reminder

By contrast, notifying a user about a particular issue through a narrative delivered by human, particularly a real human who is close to the user—not a device—makes our lives flourish more because the notification explores human relationships and makes us aware of people's empathy. We call notifications that make the user empathize others and that increase the flourishing of his/her daily life *mindful notifications*, which may provide the user with an opportunity to feel grateful for someone else and to be aware of their hospitality. *Mindful Reminder* is the fourth case study that offers mindful notifications to the user. *Mindful Reminder* aims to help the user overcome many problems in his/her daily life. For instance, it reminds the user of his/her schedule, displays information or prevents the user from forgetting objects. These mindful notifications are provided by a virtual human; they are not inorganic notifications from peripheral environments. Of course, the use of mindful and calm notifications entails a tradeoff with regard to human cognitive overload. As shown in [14], this balance is important to effectively increase the influence on the user's daily behavior through notifications via the tradeoff between his/her cognitive overload and the promotion of human relationships.

With *Mindful Reminder*, a virtual human who represents a real acquaintance of the user delivers mindful notifications. Notifications are virtualized based on the Alternative Reality concept [8]; thus, a user does not notice that the real acquaintance is not the virtual human; thus, the user believes that the notification is delivered from the real acquaintance who notifies him/her. When using *Mindful Reminder*, the user wears an HMD and the virtualized acquaintances are displayed in real space (see Figure 7). The Alternative Reality concept makes it possible to seamlessly blend virtuality into the real world. The virtualized acquaintance and the contents of the notification are chosen according to the current real location and situation of the user. Figure 8 (a) shows a typical situation in *Mindful Reminder*, where a virtualized acquaintance talks about a user's umbrella, which he/she brings with him/her on the train that he/she is riding on. Figure 8 (b) shows another example in which a shop assistant informs the user about how to stay in the café, and Figure 8 c) depicts when a user's friend talks about the class that he/she is taking in his/her school.

Two key issues are essential when designing *Mindful Reminder*. The first issue concerns the appropriate virtualized acquaintance delivering the correct information based on the user's current situation. The context awareness of the service allows us to naturally integrate a mindful notification into the real world. The second issue relates to when a user cannot recognize the difference between the real acquaintance and the virtualized acquaintance. If the user knows that the notification is delivered by a system instead of a human, the notification will not trigger an empathetic reaction from the user. The user needs to believe that the virtualized acquaintance is a real acquaintance and to be aware of the acquaintance's hospitality; the user will thus become aware of other people's hospitality toward him/her.

IV. EXPLORING DESIGN SPACE FOR DESIGNING REALITY

The guideline that we propose in this section complements the potential pitfall to incorporate virtuality in the real space based on the concept of the *magic circle* [11]. This concept has been developed to discuss the boundaries between the real space and the virtual space in video games. An expert who have designed and developed the case studies mainly charged a process to derive the guideline because he was also involved into the design and the evaluation of all case studies. The expert analysis is promising to derive abstract design knowledge. In the compiling process to extract the guideline, he generalizes and structures the ad-hoc design process to develop the case studies based on his observations. The development of the guideline was evolved in an iterated way until he had confidence that the guideline become sufficiently mature.

The proposed guideline considers that the following three levels of the magic circle are classified. The first one is the *individual magic circle*, where only one person who is a stakeholder of a service can feel the reality of an incorporated virtual value in a dimension. The second one is the *community magic circle*, where people who are members of a community as stakeholders of a service can feel the reality of an incorporated virtual value in the real space, but other people who are not the members of the

Figure 8. Illustrations of the scenarios in Mindful Reminder

community may not feel this reality. Finally, the third magic circle is the *universal magic circle*, where all people as stakeholders of a service feel the reality of an incorporated virtual value in the real space; thus, the magic circle disappears for them. These levels are crucial when considering the stakeholders in a ubiquitous computing service that incorporates virtuality, e.g., those who can sense the reality of an element in each dimension. For example, the point is frequently used in typical video games, and it can be used to strengthen a player's abilities in the game within the individual magic circle. However, the point can be usually exchanged within the game in the community magic circle, and the effect of the point is extended to most players in the game. Finally, the point can be exchanged for real money within the universal magic circle, and the effect of the point can be extended to all people.

When designing or analyzing a digital service, the levels of the magic circle become an important criterion for defining the boundaries between the real and the virtual. In particular, analyzing the levels of the service is critical when discussing the quality of the virtuality because the boundaries between the real and the virtual should be consistent among the stakeholders in the service. If a stakeholder involved in the service does not sense the reality of some of the incorporated virtual values in a dimension, incorporated virtuality has failed to affect them because the consistency among stakeholders is broken and the misunderstanding caused by the inconsistency significantly reduces the quality of the service. However, the universal magic circle is difficult to achieve because people who may not be involved in the service need to believe in the reality of some incorporated virtual values. Thus, the three levels proposed in the guideline are useful when analyzing the balance of the reality of incorporated virtuality in the digital service and the tradeoff in choosing the level.

For example, when *HoloMoL* is used by multiple users, they should see the same augmented information on the same real space if they are collaborating together. Also, in *Ambient Bot*, when a user looks at a virtual creature, other people should be aware what the user is looking at. In *Augmented Bike*, a user needs to see other bikes and pedestrians because even the user drives his/her bike in the virtual space to maintain the safety. In *Mindful Reminder*, a user's friend should be aware of the existence of the virtual persons who gives the user notifications.

From our experiences with building the four case studies described in Section III, we found that designers typically consider only individual magic circles based on their own past experiences. Therefore, in their user studies, their participants failed to understand the meaning of virtuality intended by the designers. One of important insights extracted from the discussions is that participatory design [21] is a useful tool to overcome the potential pitfalls to offer community magic circle or universal magic circle. If users who have various backgrounds are involved in the design of virtuality, the meaning of the virtuality can become understandable by them. The guideline presented in the section lets designers who develop ubiquitous computing services that incorporate virtuality to consider who are stakeholders of the services and how virtuality should be seen by these stakeholders.

Different from other guidelines and frameworks described in Section II, our framework offers design frames that allow service designers to focus on the plausibility of incorporated virtuality in the services that they develop. Especially, one important aspect of the proposed guideline is to allow service designers to explicitly take into account multiple stakeholders appeared in the services. Then, the framework is useful to find some potential pitfalls that are not easy to be extracted by other existing guidelines and frameworks.

V. CONCLUSION AND FUTURE DIRECTION

The paper presented four case studies that refine the meaning of the real space through incorporated virtuality. The case studies use HMDs to refine a user' view to include virtuality in the real space. Since the refined view significantly influences a user's behavior, the approach offers promising possibilities to develop various new services. However, as shown in Section IV, the reality needs to be properly designed in terms of who are stakeholders of the services. In particular, the services may lose the usefulness if some of stakeholders are not aware of the meaning of incorporated virtuality in an adequate manner.

The aim of this paper is to extract an effective guideline to design virtuaity from the case studies that we have developed. We hope that the guideline is useful to extract some potential pitfalls that existing guidelines and frameworks could not find easily. However, we still need to validate the proposed guideline in developing new case studies. In particular, we will plan to report actual potential pitfalls when designing the new case studies through participatory design with the proposed guideline. In the participatory design, participants will play roles of respective stakeholders in them, and discuss the meaning of incorporated virtuality from each stakeholder's angle.

REFERENCES

[1] Accenture Technology, "Mixed reality brings real benefits to enterprises", https://www.accenture.com/us-en/insight-real-benefits-mixed-reality-brings-enterprise, [retrieved: December 2017]

[2] S. Bakker and K. Niemantsverdriet, "The Interaction-Attention Continuum: Considering Various Levels of Human Attention in Interaction Design", International Journal of Design, Vol. 10, No. 2, 2016, pp.1-14.

[3] J. Baudrillard, "The Consumer Society: Myths and Structures", Sage Publications Ltd., 1998

[4] J.H. Crawford, "Carfree Cities", Intl Books, 2000

[5] A. Colley, J. Väyrynen, and J. Häkkilä, "Skiing in a blended virtuality: an in-the-wild experiment", In Proceeding of the 19th International Academic Mindtrek Conference, 2005, pp.89-91.

[6] H. Fraker, "The Hidden Potential of Sustainable Neighborhoods: Lessons from Low-Carbon Communities", Island Press, 2013

[7] N. Foletta and J. Henderson, Low Car(bon) Communities: Inspiring Car-free and Car-lite Urban Futures, Routledge, 2016

[8] F. Ishizawa and T. Nakajima, "Alternative Reality: An Augmented Daily Urban World Inserting Virtual Scenes Temporally", In Proceeding of the 10th International Conference on Ubiquitous Computing, 2016, pp.353-364.

[9] Magic Leap, https://www.magicleap.com/ [retrieved: December 2017]

[10] Microsoft HoloLens, https://www.microsoft.com/microsoft-hololens/ [retrieved: December 2017]

[11] M. Montola, J. Stemros, and A. Waern, "Pervasive Games - Theory and Design", Morgan Kaufmann, 2009.

[12] T. Nakajima and V. Lehdonvirta, "Designing Motivation in Persuasive Ambient Mirrors", Personal and Ubiquitous Computing, Vol. 17, No.1, Springer Verlag, 2013, pp.107-126.

[13] T. Narumi, Y. Ban, T. Kajinami, T. Tanikawa, and M. Hirose, "Augmented Perception of Satiety: Controlling Food Consumption by Changing Apparent Size of Food with Augmented Reality", In Proceedings of the Conference on Human Factors in Computing Systems, 2012, pp.109-118.

[14] K. Niedderer, et al., "Design for Behaviour Change as a Driver for Sustainable Innovation: Challenges and Opportunities for Implementation in the Private and Public Sectors", International Journal of Design, Vol. 10, No. 2, 2016, pp.67-85

[15] T. Okoshi, K. Tsubouchi, M. Taji, T. Ichikawa, and H. Tokuda, "Attention and Engagement-Awareness in the Wild: A Large-Scale Study with Adaptive Notifications", In Proceedings of the International Conference on Pervasive Computing and Communications, IEEE, 2017, pp.100-110.

[16] M. de Sá and E. Churchill, "Mobile augmented reality: exploring design and prototyping techniques", In Proceedings of the 14th international conference on Human-computer interaction with mobile devices and services, 2012, pp.221-230.

[17] M. Sakamoto, T. Alexandrova, and T. Nakajima, "Introducing virtuality to enhance game-related physical artifacts", International Journal of Smart Home, Vol. 8, No. 2, 2014, pp.137-152.

[18] M. Sakamoto, T. Nakajima, and T. Alexandrova, "Enhancing Values through Virtuality for Intelligent Artifacts that Influence Human Attitude and Behavior", Multimedia Tools and Applications, Springer, Vol. 74, No. 24, Springer Verlag, 2015, pp. 11537–11568

[19] M. Sakamoto and T. Nakajima, "Making Citizens' Activities Flourish through a Crowdsourcing-based Social Infrastructure", In Konomi. S., Rousso, G., (eds.) Enriching Urban Spaces with Ambient Computing, the Internet of Things, and Smart City Design, IGI Global, 2016, pp.232-255.

[20] M. Sakamoto, T. Nakajima, and S. Akioka, "Gamifying Collective Human Behavior with Gameful Digital Rhetoric", Multimedia Tools and Applications, Vol.76, No.10, Springer Verlag, 2017, pp.12539–12581

[21] D. Schuler and A. Namioka, "Participatory Design: Principles and Practices", CRC Press, 1993.

[22] E. Suzuki, T. Narumi, S. Sakurai, T. Tanikawa, and M. Hirose, "Illusion Cup: Interactive Controlling of Beverage Consumption Based on an Illusion of Volume Perception", In Proceedings of the 5th Augmented Human International Conference, 2014, Article No.41.

[23] R. Wetzel, R. McCall, A-K. Braun, and W. Broll, "Guidelines for designing augmented reality games", In Proceedings of the 2008 Conference on Future Play: Research, Play, Share, 2008.

[24] A.K. Wolfe, E.L. Malone, J. Heerwagen, and J. Dion, "Behavioral Change and Building Performance: Strategies for Significant, Persistent, and Measurable Institutional Change", US Department of Energy, 2014

[25] T. Yamabe and T. Nakajima, "Playful Training with Augmented Reality Games: Case Studies Toward Reality-oriented System Design". Multimedia Tools and Application, Vol.62, No.1, Springer Verlag, 2013, pp.259–286.

[26] F.A. Yates, "The Art of Memory", Bodley Head, 2014.

A Generic Measurement Model for Service-based Systems

Andreas Hausotter, Arne Koschel
University of Applied Sciences & Arts Hannover
Faculty IV, Department of Computer Science,
Hannover, Germany
email: Andreas.Hausotter@hs-hannover.de
email: Arne.Koschel@hs-hannover.de

Johannes Busch, Malte Zuch
University of Applied Sciences & Arts Hannover
Faculty IV, Department of Computer Science,
Hannover, Germany
email: Johannes.Busch@stud.hs-hannover.de
email: Malte.Zuch@hs-hannover.de

Abstract—**The transfer of historically grown monolithic software architectures into modern service-oriented architectures creates a lot of loose coupling points. This can lead to an unforeseen system behavior and can significantly impede those continuous modernization processes, since it is not clear where bottlenecks in a system arise. It is therefore necessary to monitor such modernization processes with an adaptive monitoring concept in order to be able to correctly record and interpret unpredictable system dynamics. For this purpose, a general measurement methodology and a specific implementation concept are presented in this work.**

Keywords–Quality of Service; Indicator Measurement; XML-Model; Service-orientation; SOA

I. INTRODUCTION

The background of this work is cooperation with a partner of the German insurance industry and their IT-Architecture. Many IT-driven and data-driven companies face the challenge of continually modernizing their infrastructure, technologies, systems and processes. The insurance industry in particular is characterized by the fact that extensive digitization of processes took place very early. This was done well before researching modern service-based approaches, such as 'traditional' service-oriented architectures (SOA) or even microservices (MS) and without the use of distributed infrastructures such as cloud computing. Historically grown software monoliths were state of the art. The modernization of such monoliths in the direction of service-based architectures is a major challenge. This conversion process is the main motivation of this work and will be explained in more detail below.

A. Motivation

Systems cannot be abruptly switched off and replaced by new architectures, but must be continuously transformed into modern architectural forms. In this continuous modernization process, monolithic structures are broken down and distributed into services. This gives companies more agility and adaptability to changing business requirements. However, a decentralized and service-oriented system architecture is usually quite fine-granular and loosely coupled. Generally, this provokes an unpredictable dynamic system behavior. This also applies to our partner in the insurance industry. In order to remain competitive, the insurance industry has to respond quickly to customer information portals, such as check24.de, where different insurance companies competetively can offer, e.g., car insurances. This scenario motivates the need for a holistic measurement concept and defines the general application scenario of this work.

So there is a fundamental need for information about the system behavior. Relevant information is collected in the 'Information Product', which represents the output of the 'Core Measurement Process' (cf. Fig. 1). The 'Information Need' provides the input for the subprocess 'Plan the Measurement Process', the subprocess 'Perform the Measurement Process' generates the Information Product'. The process goal is to satisfy the 'Information Need'.

Nowadays it is normal that customers are demanding online services unpredictably and with high volatility. These volatile demands may lead to bottlenecks in distributed service-oriented architectures. Therefore, a reliable measurement of the whole system behavior is necessary in order to eliminate any bottlenecks. Such a measurement concept and its prototypical implementation are the core contributions of our work.

B. Contribution

In order to monitor individual system components with respect to time behavior, fixed time limits have so far been used. These fixed time limits are often used in historically grown software systems of the German insurance industry. If a system component (service) could not respond within these time limits, this was interpreted as a bad quality feature. However, with these static limits, a dynamic system behavior can be poorly monitored and interpreted. The challenge is to determine, when dynamic systems are overloaded. In this

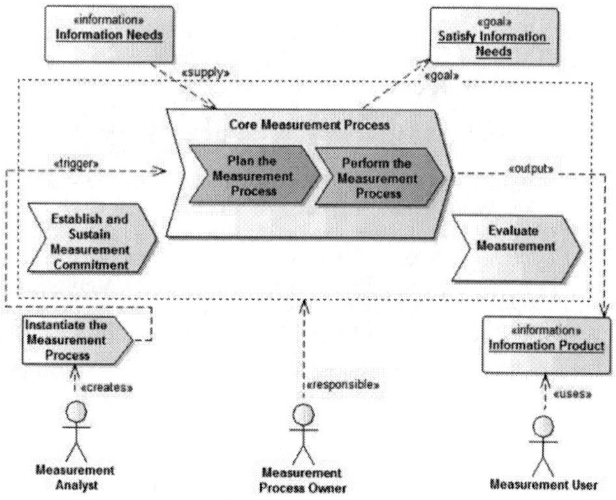

Figure 1. The Core Measurement Process

respect, a partner company of the insurance industry demands to integrate a metric, which could replace their static time limits in the future with a more dynamic metric. The general requirements lead to the following questions:

- How could static rules and timeouts be supplemented by a dynamic measurement metric?
- How could the measuring system be build on existing XML-Standards?

In previous work [1] [2], we have already developed a framework for dynamically measuring the service response time as a Quality of Service (QoS) Parameter within service-oriented architectures. As a significant enhancement to this previous work, our core contributions here are implementation details of the dynamic measuring system. Our measuring system considers existing XML standards and can flexibly record the load behavior of a software system. This measuring system should measure the response time as a particular QoS parameter as an example.

The measuring system should be able to consider both dynamic limits as well as static limits (optional). Normally, only the dynamic limits should be considered. But, if a service exceeds a fixed limit of, e.g., 5 seconds, then this should also be recognized. Another requirement is that the measuring system should 'inject' measurement agents into a software system as flexible and automated as possible. Implementation details hereof are also contributions of this article.

In Section II, related work concerning the topic of measurement models of service-based systems is explained. The measurement process with its core concepts and the information model are described in Section III and more implementation details in Section IV. Some mathematical equation explains the general measurement concept. After clarifying the general measurement plan, Section V shows how the planned measurement concept can be applied for detecting the so called 'Spikes', situations of high system-loads. The final Section VI will summarize this work. The different advantages and disadvantages of the described measurement model will be discussed. Also, an outlook to future work will show how the results of this work will be used in upcoming work in Section VI.

II. Prior and Related Work

In prior work, we already discussed several aspects of the combination of SOA, Business Process Management (BPM), Workflow Management Systems (WfMS), Business Rules Management (BRM), and Business Activity Monitoring (BAM) [3][4][5] as well as Distributed Event Monitoring and Distributed Event-Condition-Action (ECA) rule processing [6][7]. Building on this experience, we now address the area of QoS measurement for combined BRM, BPM, and SOA environments, mainly but not limited to, within the (German) insurance domain.

Work related to our research falls into several categories. We will discuss these categories in sequence.

General work on (event) monitoring has a long history (cf. [8][9] or the ACM DEBS conference series for overviews). Monitoring techniques in such (distributed) event based systems are well understood, thus such work can well contribute general monitoring principles to the work presented here. This also includes commercial solutions, such as the Dynatrace [10] system or open source monitoring software like, for example, the NAGIOS [11] solution. In these systems there is, however, generally no focus on QoS measurement within SOAs. Also, they usually do not take application domain specific requirements into account (as we do with the insurance domain).

Active Database Management Systems (ADBMS) offer some elements for use in our work (see [12][13] for overviews). Event monitoring techniques in ADBMSs are partially useful, but concentrate mostly on monitoring ADBMS internal events, and tend to neglect external and heterogeneous event sources. A major contribution of ADBMSs is their very well defined and proven semantics for definition and execution of Event-Condition-Action (ECA) rules. This leads to general classifications for parameters and options in ADBMS core functionality [13]. We may capture options that are relevant to event monitoring within parts of our general event model. QoS aspects are handled within ADBMS, for example, within the context of database transactions. However, since ADBMSs mostly do not concentrate on heterogeneity (and distribution), let alone SOAs, our research work extends into such directions.

The closest relationship to our research is the work, which directly combines the aspects QoS and SOA. As many as 2002 several articles fall into this category. However, in almost all known articles the SOA part focuses on WS-* technologies. This is in contrast to our work, which takes the operational environment of our insurance industry partners into account.

Examples of Webservice (WS-*) related QoS work include QoS-based dynamic service bind [14][15], related WS-* standards such as WS-Policy [16], and general research questions for QoS in SOA environments [17]. Design aspects and models for QoS and SOA are, for example, addressed in [14][18][19][20][21]. As for WS-* Web services, we also take XML as foundational modelling language for our work. SOA performance including QoS is discussed in articles [22], and monitoring for SOA in articles such as [23][24][25][26].

Uniqueness of our research is, that it takes all the above mentioned aspects into account. We provide a detailed XML based measurement model, as well as a generator-supported, generic SOA monitoring framework. All of it takes especially the operational environment of our insurance industry partners into account, which is a large scale SOA, but only partially WS-* technology based. This makes our work highly relevant in practice. Even more, since we base our modelling on standards, which are highly relevant for German insurance businesses (cf. VAA [27], ISO/IEC 9126 [28][29]), our work is of a quite general nature and thus can be transferable (at least within the insurance domain).

III. Plan the Measurement Process

The Core Measurement Process can be divided into two parts. First of all, the planning of the measurements takes place, which determines how the Information Need can be answered. In the second part, the planned methods of measurement will be implemented.

A. Core Concepts of the Abstract Information Model

To measure the response time behavior of a dynamic system, the definition of static response time limits is often not sufficient. When a system component (service) is deployed in a different hardware environment or in a different cloud environment, this will affect the response time of this system component. Static limits would have to be adapted manually to the new execution environment of the services. Furthermore, individual services share hardware resources with many other services. This can lead to an unpredictable system behavior, especially in complex business processes. Therefore Static limits are not sufficient, but a more flexible solution is required. The approach of this work is the investigation of a measurement concept, which is more flexible and based on the standard deviation of system load of a specifiable measuring period.

The insurance industry in particular is characterized by strong seasonal fluctuations. Towards the end of the year, many customers switch their insurance contracts and are provoking high system loads. In times of such high system loads, the mentioned static limits would be continuously exceeding. The information would be lost at the time when high loads are peaking in such a strongly demanded period. It is important to know when the current system is heavily loaded. Knowledge about this information represents the so-called Information Need (Fig. 1) of our partner from the insurance industry.

To answer this Information Need, the average response time behavior μ of a system component is firstly computed for a freely definable time period. For example, on the basis of the last $n = 500$ measured response times of the services. On the basis of this, the standard deviation is calculated within this period, shown in (1):

$$s = \sqrt{\frac{\sum_{i=1}^{n}(x_i - \mu)^2}{n - 1}} \tag{1}$$

After this calculation, the current response time r of a service is set in relation to this standard deviation s. If the response time r of a currently requested service exceeds this standard deviation by the factor of 2x, this is considered as an overload situation:

$$\text{Spike detected: } r > \mu + 2 * s \tag{2}$$

This calculation takes place continuously. As soon as a service is requested again, its response time is recorded and set in relation to the last one (e.g., the last 500 measured values). It is therefore a continuous, rolling measurement. This measuring system can be applied both for very slow system components on a daily base and also to very fine-granular services that interact in the range of milliseconds.

The important fact is that the standard deviation is calculated continuously over a defined time period, and the current response time of a service is set in relation to this. Therefore the measuring system adapts to seasonal fluctuations, and it is possible to identify, which user requests (service calls) are currently very critical with respect to the general response time behavior, independently of the prevailing current load situation. This allows fast and more precise analysis of systems and less misinterpretation due to incorrectly set static time limits. This dynamic measurement concept can give a more reliable answer to the Information Need of our project partners.

B. *Mapping of the Concepts of the Information Model*

In this subsection, a QoS Information Model (QoS IM) is presented in a more detailed manner. The QoS IM is a XML document that includes values of the concepts for a given application scenario. The concepts and their relationshipts with each other are introduced in [2]). Here we focus on the implementation of the concepts.

The QoS IM is created during the planning stage when executing the subprocess 'Plan the Measurement Process', cf. Fig. 1). The XML document is used to automatically generate the QoS Platform's artefacts. The measurements results (i.e. the output of 'Perform the Measurement Process') are produced by the QoS Platform. They are persistently stored for subsequent analysis, typically in a database system.

We opted for XML as universally accepted standard that is highly flexible, platform and vendor independent and supported by a wide variety of tools. Furthermore, XML comes with a standardized schema definition language, namely XML Schema. This is a big advantage against other languages such as JSON for example.

In the QoS IM, we specify the measurement concepts for the check24.com scenario, or the Proposal Service respectively. Due to space limitation, the discussion is restricted to the following concepts (cf. [2]):

- Measurable Concept – outlines in an abstract way, how the Quality Attributes are determined to satisfy the Information Need,
- Base Measure – specifies by its Measurement Method *how* the value of Quality Attribute is to be determined,
- Derived Measure – uses one or more Base Measures or other Derived Measures, whilst the Measurement Function specifies the calculation method and thus the combination of the Measures used,
- Indicator – is a qualitative evaluation of Quality Attributes, which directly addresses the issue raised in the Information Needs.

```
<MeasurableConcept Name="Processing_Time">
 <SubCharacteristic Name="Performance"/>
 <BaseMeasure Name="t_inst"/>
 <BaseMeasure Name="t_term"/>
 <DerivedMeasure Name="t_proc"/>
 <DerivedMeasure Name="Count_StdDev_Calls"
     />
 <DerivedMeasure Name="Count_Calls"/>
 <DerivedMeasure Name="
     StdDev_Calls_Percentage"/>
 <DerivedMeasure Name="Failed_Calls"/>
</MeasurableConcept>
```

Listing 1. Calculation of the Proposal Service's Processing Time

The Measurable Concept `Processing_Time` references by name all necessary Base and Derived Measures (cf. listing 1).

The definition of the Base Measure `t_inst` is shown in listing 2. Its task is to capture the start time of a Proposal Service call (by a user request). The element `Attribute` specifies the attribute of the Proposal Service to be observed. The element hierarchy of `Implementation` defines all platform specific information to automatically generate all artefacts needed for the measurement, i.e., the agent class with attributes and the measurement method (cf. subsection IV).

```
1  <BaseMeasure Name="t_inst">
2   <Scale TypeOfScale="Rational" Type="R"/>
3   <Attribute ServiceID="BAS_001" AttributeName="ServiceCallID"/>
4   <MeasurementMethod Name="recordTimeOfServiceCall">
5   <Implementation>
6    <Agent Class="ServiceAgent">
7    <Method>
8    <Attribute Name="ServiceCallID" Type=.../>
9    <Attribute Name="Time" Type=... Computed="time"/>
10   <Event Name="ServiceStartEvent"/>
11   </Method>
12   </Agent>
13  </Implementation>
14  </MeasurementMethod>
15 </BaseMeasure>
```

Listing 2. Start Time of a Proposal Service Call

The Derived Measure `Count_StdDev_Calls` presented in listing 3 calculates the number of Proposal Service calls that exceeds twice the standard deviation (cf. subsection IV, (2)).

```
1  <DerivedMeasure Name="Count_StdDev_Calls">
2   <Uses><DerivedMeasure Name="t_proc"/></Uses>
3   <MeasurementFunction Name="calculateNumberOfCallsAboveSTDDEV">
4    <Implementation>
5     <Analyzer>
6      <Query Class="ServiceDuration" Type=...>
7       <Plain>
8       SELECT COUNT(*) FROM serviceduration
9       WHERE
10      TINTS > TIME_SECS(DATEADD('DAY',
11                  -30,NOW()))
12      AND TPROC > (SELECT AVG(TPROC)
13                        + (2 * STDDEV(TPROC))
14      FROM serviceduration
15        WHERE TINTS > TIME_SECS(
16          DATEADD('DAY',-30, NOW())))
17      </Plain>
18     </Query>
19    </Analyzer>
20   </Implementation>
21  </MeasurementFunction>
22  <UnitOfMeasurement>ms</UnitOfMeasurement>
23  <TargetValue>1</TargetValue>
24 </DerivedMeasure>
```

Listing 3. Compute the Number of Proposal Service Calls that Exceed Twice the Standard Deviation

`Count_StdDev_Calls` is based on a different Derived Measure, namely `t_proc`, which computes the processing time of a Proposal Service call (cf. `Uses` element, line 2). The element `Implementation` comprises of all information that is used to generate the analyzer class (cf. subsection IV). The analyzer executes the SQL Select statement (cf. lines 8 to 16), which represents the content of the element `Plain`. This is done by the measurement function `calculateNumberOfCallsAboveSTDDEV`, shown in line 3, whenever an event `ServiceDurationEvent` has been fired (cf. line 6).

Finally, the Indicator `SLoT_proc`, shown in listing 4, evaluates the adequacy of the processing time of all Proposal Service calls.

`SLoT_proc` is based on two different Derived Measures, namely `StdDev_Calls_Percentage`, and `Failed_Calls` respectively (cf. `Uses` element, lines 4 to 7). The first measure, `StdDev_Calls_Percentage`, takes `Count_StdDev_Calls` and `Count_Calls` and does some basic arithmetic computation.

The element `DecisionCriteria` specifies a decision table, so that a value, computed by the Derived Measures, can be mapped to the entry of the given nominal scale (i.e., high, medium, low). The element `Implementation` comprises all information to generate the analyzer class (cf. subsection IV), which implements the decision table and the mapping.

```
1  <Indicator Name="SLoT_proc">
2   <AnalysisModel Name="computeAdequacyOfProcessingTime">
3   <Scale TypeOfScale="Nominal" Type=.../>
4   <Uses>
5   <DerivedMeasure Name="StdDev_Calls_Percentage"/>
6   <DerivedMeasure Name="Failed_Calls"/>
7   </Uses>
8   <DecisionCriteria>
9   <Implementation>
10   <Analyzer>
11   <IndicatorTable Class="IndicatorController" Type="HMN">
12   <IndicatorEntry>
13   <Input>devPercentageCount < 5 && badCount == 0</Input>
14   <Result>low</Result>
15   </IndicatorEntry>
16   ...
17   </IndicatorTable>
18   </Analyzer>
19  </Implementation>
20  </DecisionCriteria>
21  </AnalysisModel>
22 </Indicator>
```

Listing 4. Compute the Adequacy of the Processing Time of all Proposal Service Calls

IV. CONCEPTS IMPLEMENTATION BASED ON GENERATORS

The initial phases of applying an IM (cf. Fig. 2) were shown in Section III-B. This section discusses subsequent phases (especially about generators, artefacts, etc.) in detail. Please note, although its concepts are transferable, our QoS Generator aims not to be of generic nature, but is tailored specifically towards our XML based IM and needs of our partner companies. Furthermore, the generated artefacts are specific to our current QoS Platform. Both offer the flexibility to tailor each part to the specific needs of each of our partner companies.

A. Design of the QoS Generator

Several different artefacts have to be generated to apply a specific IM. The basic design of the QoS Generator is

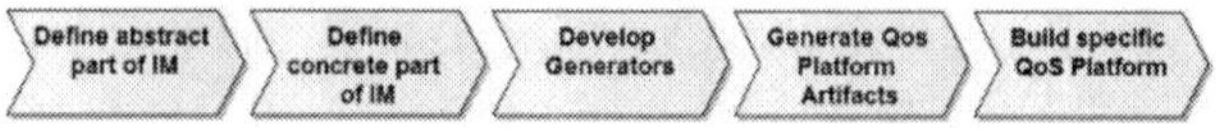

Figure 2. Phase from IM to QoS System.

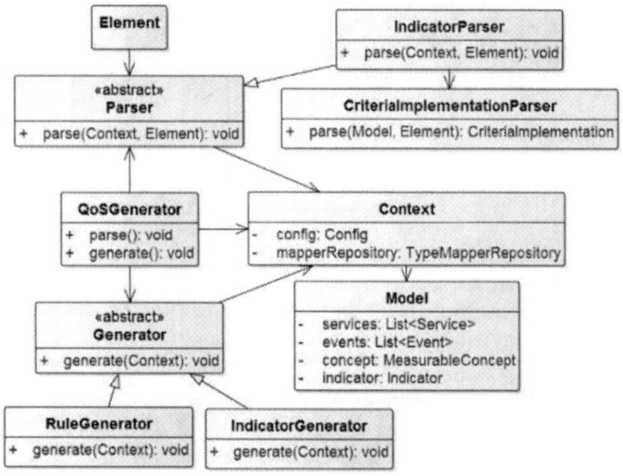

Figure 3. Design of the QoS Generator.

given in Fig. 3. In general, it consists of a parser step and a generator step. Purpose of the first step is to build an optimized in-memory model of an IM. A parser gets the XML root element and parses the abstract part (as shown through the IndicatorParser) and then the concrete part (as shown by the CriteriaImplementationParser). This distinction is necessary for the desired flexibility of the QoS Platform itself.

The optimized model is part of the Context class and given to each generator as part of the second step. Also, the Context contains general configuration information and a TypeMapperRepository. This latter contains mappers to translate XML types into implementation specific types (e.g., SQL, Java, etc.).

While the parsers are tailored towards the IM model, the generators are tailored towards implementation artefacts or concepts. Hence, there are generators for the QoS Agent, Indicator implementation or complex event processing (CEP) rules. Each generator has a specific task concluding in the generation of certain artefacts. This further supports the flexibility of the QoS Platform itself.

B. Implemented concepts and their artefacts

In the following paragraphs, different concrete parts and their corresponding artefacts are presented. Note, only excerpts are shown and currently not all elements of the abstract part are used.

The concrete part of the Base Measure `t_inst` is given in Listing 2. It defines `Attribute` elements and references the computed QoS Event. The ServiceCallID is parsed from Service Call data. The Time attribute will be computed through the Agent itself. Furthermore, a class attribute is given in the Agent element. It is used to structure the generated code and the corresponding artefacts. The specific method name is derived from the `MeasurementMethod` element.

The concrete part of the Derived Measure `t_proc` is given in Listing 5. It contains the definition of the CEP rule, which computes the complex event ServiceDurationEvent. Plain element indicates that this code fragment will be placed "as is" into a rule file. Only import definitions (e.g., for event classes) will be added. The rule file is loaded on start up by the CEP engine (JBoss Drools) of the QoS Measurement module.

```
<Rule>
 <Event Name="ServiceDurationEvent"
  Handle="output"/>
 <Plain>
  rule "Service Duration Rule"
  when
   $start : ServiceStartEvent()
   $end : ServiceEndEvent(
    this after[ 0s , 2s ] $start &&
    this.id == $start.id
   )
  then
   channels["analyzer"].send(
    new ServiceDurationEvent(...)
   );
  end
 </Plain>
</Rule>
```

Listing 5. Concrete Part of a Rule.

The concrete part of the Derived Measure `COUNT_STDEV_CALLS` is given in Listing 3. It contains the SQL query to get the count of all events with a runtime above the doubled standard deviation. The generated class is shown in Listing 6. The query attribute contains the SQL query of the Plain element. Again, the class attribute is used to structure the code and artefacts, but the Type attribute is specific for a query and specifies the return type (in this case Long) of the query. The name of method is given in the `MeasurementFunction` element. Furthermore, needed imports and Spring code to integrate the jdbcOperations object are generated.

```
public class ServiceDurationQuery {
 ...
 public Long
     calculateNumberOfCallsAboveSTDDEV() {
   return jdbcOperations.queryForObject(
     query, Long.class );
 }
}
```

Listing 6. Generated query class.

The concrete part of the Indicator `SLoT_proc` is given in Listing 4. Each `IndicatorEntry` element consists of an `Input` where the Indicator condition is defined and a `Result` element, which contains the actual Indicator response. Each of these results have to be a valid HMN type. The generated IndicatorController class is given in Listing 7. The dependencies to other Measure results are given through the `Uses` element. This information is also used for generation and manual modifications.

While the QoS Agent is only designed as part of the QoS System, it is actually placed directly into the SOA as part of the ESB.war. The used ESB is a partner specific implementation. The generated class and rule files for the DerivedMeasures are part of the QoS Platform (and part of the QoS Platform.war). For example, the generated classes of

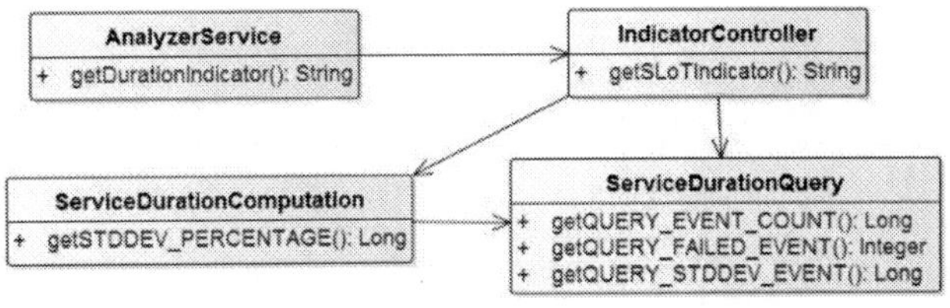

Figure 4. Detailed view into the Analyzer Module.

the Analyzer module are shown in Fig. 4. Indicator and *-Duration classes are integrated, if needed manually, onto the QoS Platform. The AnalyzerService class is considered part of the QoS Platform core and implements the REST interface for downstream systems (e.g., alerting).

```
public class IndicatorController {
 public String
     computeAdequacyOfProcessingTime() {
  ...
  if(devPercentageCount < 5 &&
     badCount == 0) {
   return "niedrig";
  }
  if(devPercentageCount >= 5 &&
     badCount == 0) {
   return "mittel";
  } else {
   return "hoch";
  }
}}
```

Listing 7. Generated indicator class.

V. MEASUREMENTS

For the evaluation of the described measurement concept, it is stressed with an initial load test. The general 'Information Need' (Fig. 1) is the information about how volatile a software system is currently being stressed. Static thresholds cannot fulfill the desired 'Information Need' of the partner companies in the insurance industry. The dynamic approach of measuring the spikes, which exceed the standard-deviation of a measuring period, can provide better answers here. For the evaluation, such spikes are directly provoked. When generating the spikes, two parameters are randomly influenced:

- Intensity: The intensity of the spikes.
- Frequency: The frequency at which the spikes occur.

In the stress test, the two parameters 'Intensity' and 'Frequency' are set. A high intensity means that a spike is generated with a high level of volatility. The intensity describes, how long the response time of a service request is and how 'intensive' the standard deviation is exceeded according to (1). The frequency determines, how often such a spike should occur in the stress test. The stress test therefore generates very volatile measurement events, which must be recorded dynamically by the measuring system. So, a random variation of these two parameters will provoke volatile stress situations with unpredictable intensity and frequency. This allows the measuring system to be tested as strongly and dynamically as possible. Some of the preliminary results measured with the QoS System are shown in Fig. 5. The yellow line shows the

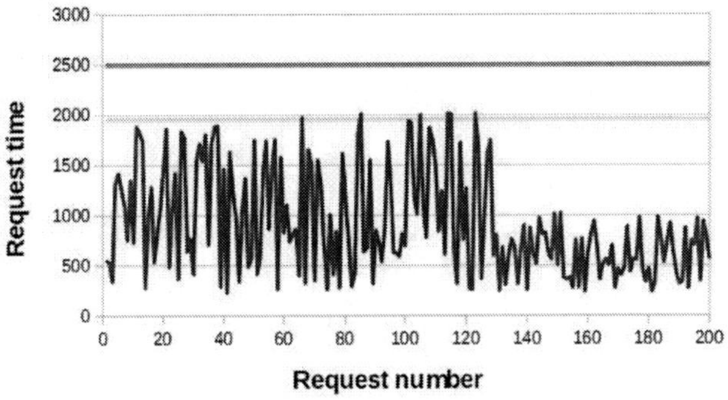

Figure 5. Preliminary Measurement Results.

standard deviation barrier. In this case, 3 % of all measured requests (6 service calls) are violating the barrier, thus the computed indicator would be low. Above 5 % the indicator would be middle. The red line shows the SLA barrier introduced by service consumers like check24.de. If one request exceeds this barrier the indicator switches to high. A more thorough test and evaluation based on these loads will be given in our future work. But based on these results, the measurement concept can be used to even measure very volatile stress situations

VI. CONCLUSION AND FUTURE WORK

In this article we presented an approach for monitoring a distributed SOA environment, which we see as a promising path to take. Our SOA Quality Model is aimed to follow the ISO/IEC-Standard 15939 (cf. [30]), which enables a wide range of use cases. Our Measurement Concept outlines an execution platform for the specific QoS Information Model, which should cause minimal impact on the SOA environment.

The separation of Measurement Agents and QoS-Analyzer on one hand allows lightweight agents and on the other hand a very capable analyzer component. Furthermore certain parts of our QoS Platform can be replaced or complemented with common tools, e.g., from the microservices eco system. For example, Netflix's Hystrix could be used to implement a BaseMeasure or Prometheus to implement DerivedMeasures. This flexibility in our architecture with the general concept given through our SOA Quality Model offers new opportunities for our partner companies.

Already in previous work [1] [2] we presented our general measurement concept, an initial business process (the 'check 24' Proposal Service insurance use case, a basic business relevant scenario), and our information model and concept. The core contributions of the present article are implementation details of our approach. Therefore in Section III we dive deeply into our information model and in Section IV our model-driven, generator based implementation is described in depth.

Our ongoing work of applying the QoS System to an application scenario relevant to our partner in the insurance industry (the so called 'Check 24 process'), will provide evidence of the practical usability of the created framework. It is expected, that our monitoring system will help to discover potential bottlenecks in the current system design of our partner's distributed services. Therefore, it will create value in the process of solving these issues.

In future work, we have planned to apply our existing work to the more complex insurance process 'Angebot erstellen' ('create individual proposal') of the VAA [27]. Thus, we will implement a more complex insurance scenario. Moreover, the actual measurement and analysis of the results are an ongoing process, which is yet to be finished.

We also have plans to apply these results onto cloud based environments. Furthermore, a deeper subdivision or extraction from the current coarse granular SOA services into more fine grained microservices will be investigated by us in future work 'where it makes sense', for example, to allow for a better scalability of individual microservices.

REFERENCES

[1] A. Hausotter, A. Koschel, J. Busch, M. Petzsch, and Malte Zuch, "Implementing a Framework for QoS Measurement in SOA", submitted for publication, 2017.

[2] A. Hausotter, A. Koschel, J. Busch, M. Petzsch, and Malte Zuch, "Agent based Framework for QoS Measurement Applied in SOA," in: The 9th International Conferences on Advanced Service Computing (Service Computation), IARIA, Athens, Greece, 2017, pp. 16-23.

[3] T. Bergemann, A. Hausotter, and A. Koschel, "Keeping Workflow-Enabled Enterprises Flexible: WfMS Abstraction and Advanced Task Management," in: 4th Int. Conference on Grid and Pervasive Computing Conference (GPC), 2009, pp. 19-26.

[4] C. Gäth, et al., "Always Stay Agile! – Towards Service-oriented Integration of Business Process and Business Rules Management," in: The Sixth International Conferences on Advanced Service Computing (Service Computation), IARIA, Venice, Italy, 2014, pp. 40-43.

[5] A. Hausotter, C. Kleiner, A. Koschel, D. Zhang, and H. Gehrken, "Always Stay Flexible! WfMS-independent Business Process Controlling in SOA," in: IEEE EDOCW 2011: Workshops Proc. of the 15th IEEE Intl. Enterprise Distributed Object Computing Conference, IEEE: Helsinki, Finnland, 2011, pp. 184-193.

[6] A. Koschel and R. Kramer, "Configurable Event Triggered Services for CORBA-based Systems," Proc. 2nd Intl. Enterprise Distributed Object Computing Workshop (EDOC'98), San Diego, U.S.A, 1998, pp. 1-13.

[7] M. Schaaf, I. Astrova, A. Koschel, and S. Gatziu, "The OM4SPACE Activity Service - A semantically well-defined cloud-based event notification middleware," in: IARIA Intl. Journal On Advances in Software, 7(3,4), 2014, pp. 697-709.

[8] B. Schroeder, "On-Line Monitoring: A Tutorial," IEEE Computer, 28(6), pp. 72-80, 1995.

[9] S. Schwiderski, "Monitoring the Behavior of Distributed Systems," PhD thesis, Selwyn College, University of Cambridge, University of Cambridge, Computer Lab, Cambridge, United Kingdom, 1996.

[10] Dynatrace LLC, "Dynatrace Application Monitoring," [Online]. URL: https://www.dynatrace.com/de/products/application-monitoring.html [accessed: 2017-12-06].

[11] Nagios.ORG, "Nagios Core Editions," [Online]. URL: https://www.nagios.org/ [accessed: 2016-12-26].

[12] N. W. Paton (ed.), "Active Rules for Databases," Springer, New York, 1999.

[13] ACT-NET Consortium, "The Active DBMS Manifesto," ACM SIGMOD Record, 25(3), 1996.

[14] M. Garcia-Valls, P. Basanta-Val, M. Marcos, and E. Estévez, "A bi-dimensional QoS model for SOA and real-time middleware," in: Intl. Journal of Computer Systems Science and Engineering, CLR Publishing, 2013, pp. 315-326.

[15] V. Krishnamurthy and C. Babu, "Pattern Based Adaptation for Service Oriented Applications," in: ACM SIGSOFT Softw. Eng. Notes 37, 2012(1), 2012, pp. 1-6.

[16] T. Frotscher, G. Starke (ed.), and S. Tilkov (ed.), "Der Webservices-Architekturstack," in: SOA-Expertenwissen, Heidelberg, dpunkt.verlag, 2007, pp. 489-506.

[17] F. Curbera, R. Khalaf, and N. Mukhi, "Quality of Service in SOA Environments. An Overview and Research Agenda," in: it - Information Technology 50, 2008(2), 2008, pp. 99-107.

[18] S.W. Choi, J.S. Her, and S.D. Kim, "QoS Metrics for Evaluating Services from the Perspective of Service Providers," in: Proc. of the IEEE International Conference on e-Business Engineering, Washington DC, USA : IEEE Computer Society (ICEBE'07), 2007, pp. 622-625.

[19] Z. Balfagih and M.F. Hassan, "Quality Model for Web Services from Multi-stakeholders' Perspective," in: Proceedings of the 2009 International Conference on Information Management and Engineering, Washington DC, USA : IEEE Computer Society (ICIME'09), 2009, pp. 287-291.

[20] G. Wang, A. Chen, C. Wang, C. Fung, and S. Uczekaj, "Integrated Quality of Service (QoS) Management in Service-Oriented Enterprise Architectures," in: Proceedings of the 8th IEEE Intl. Enterprise Distributed Object Computing Conference (EDOC'04), Washington DC, USA, IEEE, 2004, pp. 21-32.

[21] M. Varela, L. Skorin-Kapov, F. Guyard, and M. Fiedler, "Meta-Modeling QoE", PIK-Praxis der Informationsverarbeitung und Kommunikation, 2014, Vol. 37(4), pp. 265-274.

[22] R.W. Maule and W.C. Lewis, "Performance and QoS in Service-Based Systems", Proc. of the 2011 IEEE World Congress on Services, IEEE Computer Society, 2011, pp. 556-563.

[23] B. Wetzstein, et al., "Monitoring and Analyzing Influential Factors of Business Process Performance," in: Proc. IEEE Intl. Enterprise Distributed Object Computing Conf. (EDOC'09), 2009, pp. 141-150.

[24] F. Rosenberg, C. Platzer, and S. Dustdar, "Bootstrapping Performance and Dependability Attributes of Web Services," in: Proc. International Conference on Web Services (ICWS'06), 2006, pp. 205-212.

[25] M. Schmid, J. Schaefer, and R. Kroeger, "Ein MDSD-Ansatz zum QoS-Monitoring von Diensten in Serviceorientierten Architekturen," in: PIK Praxis der Informationsverarbeitung und Kommunikation, 31 (2008) 4, 2008, pp. 232-238.

[26] S.M.S. da Cruz, R.M. Costa, M. Manhaes, and J. Zavaleta, "Monitoring SOA-based Applications with Business Provenance", Proc. of the 28th Annual ACM Symposium on Applied Computing (ACM SAC), ACM, 2013, pp. 1927-1932.

[27] GDV (Gesamtverband der Deutschen Versicherungswirtschaft e.V. – General Association o.t. German Insurance Industry), "Die Anwendungsarchitektur der Versicherungswirtschaft: Das Objektorientierte Fachliche Referenzmodell (The application architecture of the German insurance business – The functional object-oriented reference model", VAA Final Edt. Vers. 2.0, 2001, [Online]. URL: http://www.gdv-online.de/vaa/vaafe_html/dokument/ofrm.pdf [accessed: 2017-01-11].

[28] ISO - International Organization for Standardization (ed.), "ISO/IEC 25010:2011 - Systems and software engineering – Systems and software Quality Requirements and Evaluation (SQuaRE) – System and software quality models", 2011.

[29] M. Azuma, "SQuaRE: the next generation of the ISO/IEC 9126 and 14598 international standards series on software product quality, " in: Proc. of European Software Control and Metrics (ESCOM), 2001, pp. 337-346.

[30] ISO - International Organization for Standardization (ed.), "ISO/IEC 15939:2007 - Systems and software engineering - Measurement process," 2007.

Digital Brain as a Service: An Approach For Achieving Organic Web Services

Islam Elgedawy
Computer Engineering Department,
Middle East Technical University, Northern Cyprus Campus
99738 Kalkanli, Guzelyurt, Mersin 10, Turkey,
Email: Elgedawy@metu.edu.tr

***Abstract*—To be able to build self-managing services, services should not be only autonomic, but also organic. This is because autonomic services can lead to services' failure when new unpredicted situations arise, as they are currently built using predefined sets of rules and policies manually tailored for specific situations and contexts. Hence, autonomic services need to support organic properties, such as self-learning and self-explanation in order to handle such unpredicted situations. Currently, all existing works focus on making services autonomic, but not organic. To overcome such limitation, this paper proposes a novel approach to build organic web services. The proposed approach aims to build digital brains as a service, which will be responsible for all cognition, thinking, learning, planning, and decision making tasks, such that any ordinary service can become organic just by plugging it to the corresponding digital brain service. The proposed approach builds the digital brain service as a composite web service, realizing the components of the adopted Starzyk-Prasad machine consciousness computational model. The proposed approach opens the doors for a new era, where digital brains for software systems can be created, trained, and rented.**

Keywords–Digital Brains; Machine Consciousness; Self-Managing systems; Organic Services.

I. Introduction

The vision of organic computing [1] was introduced to create self-managing software systems, such that different organic properties (such as self-learning, self-explanation, adaptability, steady growth, and evolution) are needed to be supported. Organic computing is an extended version of the autonomic computing vision, where software systems are required to support autonomic self-managing properties (namely, self-configuration, self-optimization, self-healing, and self-protection) [2]. Currently, existing approaches for creating autonomic systems (such as the works discussed in [3][4][5]) are limited and can lead to systems' failure [5]. This is because the design of autonomous systems is mainly based on predefined static rules and policies given by service designers during design and/or run times [5]. Hence, any situation that is not covered by such predefined rules and policies will jeopardize the system, the users, and the embodying environment to all types of problems. To overcome such problems, self-managing systems should not be only autonomic, but also organic.

Being organic means the systems will be able to learn and explain unknown concepts to themselves and to others. It also means systems should be able to sense their internal states as well as their embodying environment, rationalize about the perceived facts, predict future actions and events, decide on best actions in given situations, grow their knowledge, and able to communicate like humans. All these requirements are needed to be done without having static predefined rules and policies. The software systems after a period of training should be able to explore and learn by itself exactly as humans. This motivates the work in this paper that shows how we can create organic web services satisfying these challenging requirements.

In humans, consciousness is responsible for handling all the high-level tasks, such as cognition, thinking, learning, planning, and decision making. As these tasks are essential for having any organic property, we argue that services must have "consciousness" to be able to perform such high-level tasks. Currently, there exist many computational models for machine consciousness that try to mimic human consciousness [6][7][8]. We argue that such computational models are rich enough to model services' consciousness, as services have specific finite functionalities, and finite number of goals, which is much less complex than humans' functionalities and goals. We previously proposed to capture machine consciousness as a service (MCaaS) in [9], in which we proposed to realize the Starzyk-Prasad machine consciousness model [8]. Such MCaaS service should be able to accomplish all the cognition and thinking tasks.

In this paper, we propose a novel approach to build organic web services, as shown in Figure 1.

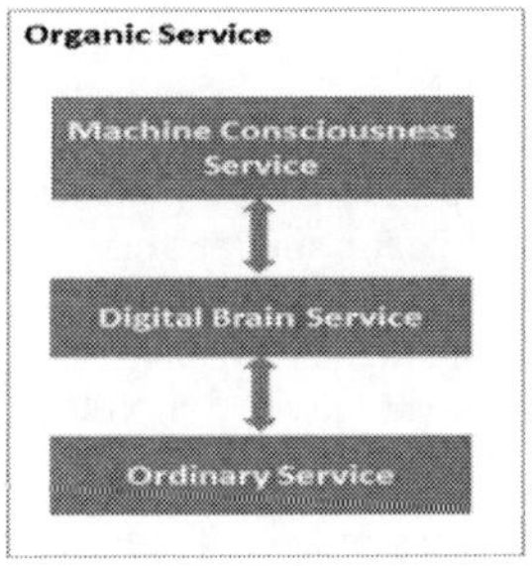

Figure 1. The proposed approach for achieving organic web services

The figure shows a digital brain service is created to directly manage the targeted services, where the digital brain service will be connected to the MCaaS service to accomplish all the cognition and thinking tasks. Adopting service-oriented computing to build software systems facilitates creation of autonomic and organic software systems, as systems' components can be encapsulated as loosely-coupled services that can be monitored and replaced at run time, as shown in the previously proposed CRESCENT framework [3]. However, to be able to realize the proposed approach, many problems need to be solved, such as the representation problem, the memory modeling problem, the planning and thinking problem, and the motivation and learning problem. We proposed different solutions for every problem adopting a collection of existing techniques; details are given in Section IV. The proposed approach for achieving organic web services opens the doors for a new era, where digital brains for software systems can be created, trained, and rented.

The rest of the paper is organized as follows. Section II summarizes the adopted Starzyk-Prasad machine consciousness model. Section III discusses the challenges for achieving organic services. Section IV provides the proposed approach for creating digital brains for organic services and provides solutions for the discussed challenges. Section V demonstrates a use case for the proposed approach. Finally, Section VI concludes the paper and provides the directions for future work.

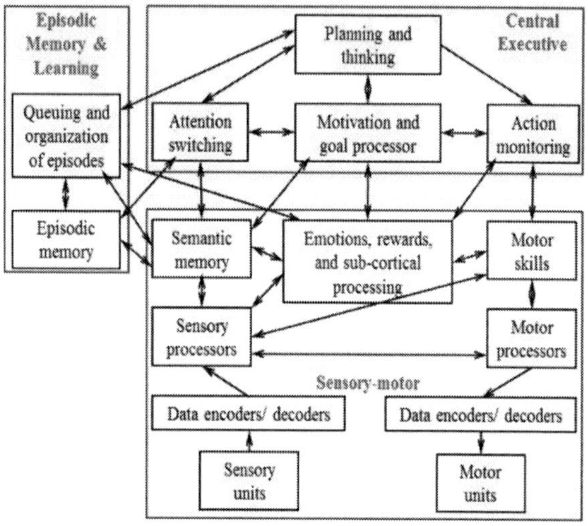

Figure 2. The Starzyk-Prasad Machine Consciousness Model [8]

II. BACKGROUND

This section provides the background required for the proposed approach. It summarizes the adopted Starzyk-Prasad machine consciousness model [8], providing their definitions for machine consciousness. The work in [7] categorized existing machine consciousness models into five categories: a global workspace, information integration, an internal self-model, higher-level representations, and attention mechanisms. As shown in [8], the Starzyk-Prasad model characteristics explicitly and implicitly cover all the above categories. This is why we chose it to model service consciousness. The Starzyk-Prasad consciousness model follows the functionalism perspective, and sees consciousness as an emergent property resulting from "the interactions between interconnected modules with attention switching mechanism helping to select a cognitive experience and managing a sequential cognitive process." [8]. They define machine consciousness as follows:

> "A machine is conscious if besides the required mechanisms for perception, action, learning and associative memory, it has a central executive that controls all the processes (conscious or subconscious) of the machine; the central executive is driven by the machine's motivation and goal selection, attention switching, semantic and episodic memory and uses cognitive perception and cognitive understanding of motivations, thoughts, or plans to control learning, attention, motivations, and monitor actions [8]."

Figure 2 depicts the architecture of the Starzyk-Prasad machine consciousness model. The figure shows that the model consists of three main modules: the sensory-motor module, the episodic memory and learning module, and the central executive module. We summarize these modules functionalities as follows:

- *Sensory-Motor Module.* It is the module responsible for collecting different sensory data. It uses such data for "concept formation", which will be used to build different types of associative memories. For example, semantic memory will store the gained knowledge about the environment), while a procedural memory will build a hierarchy of motor skills (i.e., learnt and basic actions). The module is also responsible for motor actuation , and generation of emotional and reward signals. Such signals govern the learning process and serve as an interface to other units. The sensory-motor module is composed of three parts: sensory processors integrated with semantic memory, motor processors integrated with motor skills, and sub-cortical processor integrated with emotions and rewards. In other words, it is the module responsible for the "subconscious", that automatically takes care of the actions and internal states that are previously learnt. However, it will contact the other higher consciousness modules if a conscious action is required. The sensor-motor module is connected to sensory and motor units via data encoders and decoders. Motor processor receives feedback from sensory processors. The sensory processers are the orchestrators of the sensory-motor module. They receive the inputs, contacts the semantic memory and subcortical processing modules to decide on the actions to be taken. Then, they contact the motor processors to execute the taken actions if no thinking is required.
- *Episodic Memory and Learning Module.* It is the module responsible for storing and recalling experiences, and responsible for recognizing the novel events/patterns in various processes and their semantic relationships. It is composed of two parts, episodic memory unit and learning unit. Episodic memory unit is a collection of smaller functional blocks, each dedicated to capture spatial and temporal semantic relationships of different data sequences. It stores and manages data as episodes collected from all the units including perceptions, motivations and interpretations of cognitive experiences and their significance from the central executive. Learning about specific events/patterns is directed by the central executive module.
- *Central Executive Module.* It is the module responsi-

ble for thinking, planning, coordination and selective control of all the other units. Its tasks include cognitive perception, focusing attention, attention switching, motivation, goal creation and selection, thoughts, planning, learning, etc. For this purpose, it needs the capability to dynamically select and direct execution of programs that govern attention, motivation, episodic memory and action monitoring. In addition, central executive can activate semantic memory and control emotions. Central executive module does not have a centralized decision making center. Instead, its decisions are result of competition between signals generated from units. Such signals vary in intensity based on internal or external aspects at a given moment. Once a winner is established, central executive provides cognitive interpretation of the result, providing top down activation for perception, planning, internal thought or motor functions.

The model adopts an attention switching mechanism that takes into consideration both internal and external observations. Internal observations result from changes in internal motivation, planning tasks, and components status. External observations result from opportunities, threats, and failures of the embodying environment. The cognitive realization of internal processes states decides the central executive s decision of what is observed, planning how to respond, and evaluating the created action plans. Once an action is selected to be performed, its consequences must be taken into consideration before the actual execution of the action. The model implements both attention focusing and attention switching. Selection between signals is not via a competition rather than via a conscious decision to select the signal that fulfills the current goals, based on their priorities (e.g., survival is considered the highest priority goal). Once an attention switching occurs, the system focuses its cognitive attention on the selected issue.

III. Challenges For Achieving Organic Web Services

There are four main challenges for achieving organic web services, namely, the representation problem, the memory modeling problem, the motivation and learning problem, and the planning and thinking problem. We summarize these problems as follows.

A. The Representation Problem

Representation is one of the most controversial problems in machine consciousness [10]. How do we represent a concept? How do we get its meaning knowing the physical world cannot possess any semantics? How to assign meaning to mental states?

In neuroscience, empirical evidence demonstrates that every region of the neocortex represents a given piece of information using a specific sparse activity pattern of large collection of neurons. This sparse activation pattern is grounded, which means the same group of neurons are activated every time the same symbol/concept is identified. This indicates that the current best way forward of the representation problem is to adopt distributed sparse encoding techniques [11]. Finding the suitable data representation is crucial for building the encoders/decoders, memory modules, the learning and thinking units. Currently, there exist many sparse autoencoders (SAE), for example, the work in [12] proposed different generic SAEs, for scalar data, categorical data, and date-time data. However, the work in [13] proposed a sparse encoder that learns sparsity connections rather than enforcing them as in traditional SAEs. Currently, there does not exist an SAE that performs well in all applications domains, hence the question of which sparse encoding technique should be chosen for a given application domain is left for empirical research.

B. The Memory Modeling Problem

The Starzyk-Prasad model uses different types of associative memories (e.g., semantic, episodic, and procedural). Every associative memory type is different in terms of its purpose, functionality, and architecture. Hence, a different model is needed for every memory type. In what follows, we provide a quick overview of the existing models.

- For semantic memory modeling, we can find models, such as the ones proposed in [14][15][16]. For example, the work in [14] proposed a well-known simple model for semantic memory adopting a feed-forward neural network, in which activation propagates from the inputs (concepts and relations) to the outputs (attributes) with hidden layers in between. Each unit in the input layer corresponds to an individual concept in the environment. Each unit in the relation layer represents contextual constraints on the kind of information to be retrieved. The network is trained to turn on all those units that represent correct completions of the input query. The work in [15] proposed a more complex neural model using pain networks, where sensory data, biases, pains, and actions are connected via neural network, such that each pain neuron is associated with its corresponding pain detection and learning unit, and motivates the machine to act. It adopts both forward and backward connections to determine the weights of the connections. While, the work in [16][17] proposed a new model known as hierarchial temporal memory (HTM), which is a hierarchical deep neural model adopting the human cortex structure.
- For episodic memory modeling, the work in [18]. is one of the recent proposed model, it propose to use a neural model based on fusion adaptive resonance theory. The proposed model learns episodic traces in response to a continuous stream of sensory input and feedback received from the environment. It extracts key events and encodes spatial and temporal relations between events by dynamically creating cognitive nodes. It also supports a mechanism of gradual forgetting.
- For procedural memory modeling, the work in [19] adopts a contention scheduling model that uses discrete, hierarchically-organized goal and action representations.

As we can see, each memory type has its own model that facilitate its purpose. Hence, we need to decide on the suitable model for each needed memory type, encapsulate it as service, and let it accessed via a suitable memory manager service to store and retrieve information.

C. The Motivation and Learning problem

Motivations are related to either cognitively recognized or unconscious needs and desires, emotional changes, and internally set abstract goals, hence motivation is essential for determining attention focus and attention switching tasks. Learning is essential to achieve two major tasks:

- *Concept identification*: Concept identification learning is a process that aims to extract the space-temporal relations from different internal and external sensory data. Then, it uses such information to identify different concepts and their relationships.
- *Action selection*: Action selection learning is about choosing the suitable actions to optimize different objectives originated by the adopted motivation model. Reinforcement learning is a very well known and established scheme for action selection that is only motivated by making gains (rewards). However, the work in [20] showed that the motivational learning (ML) approach proposed in [15] outperformed many of the well-known reinforcement learning approaches.

D. The Planning and Thinking Problem

One of the possible signs of having consciousness is the ability to switch attention to attend to emerging situations. Response to emerging situation depends on the adopted motivation and goal models. As per the Starzyk-Prasad model, the digital brain service needs to determine the attention spotlight in every situation in a way that reduces its pains and increases its rewards. An object/concept in the spotlight needs to be determined (usually, it is the one with the most salient features), and the most suitable action (retrieved from the corresponding associative memories) should be performed. If there is lack of certain resources needed to execute the action, the digital brain service has to search for it and plan to get it, which creates sub-goal(s) for the current goal. Hence, a suitable action plan needs to be created to fulfill the current goal and its subgoals.

IV. The Proposed Approach For Achieving Organic Web Services

This section first summarizes the proposed approach for achieving organic web services, then it introduces solutions for the discussed challenges, and finally it proposes a road map for the approach realization.

To make an ordinary service "organic", the proposed approach aims to build a digital brain service, which will be plugged into the ordinary targeted service in order to directly manage it, provided that the digital brain service will be plugged into a machine consciousness service in order to accomplish all the cognition and thinking tasks, as shown in Figure 1. We require any service that wants to use the digital brain service, to expose the suitable interfaces that enable reading the sensory data and executing the required actions. Like any machine learning approach, digital brains require some training first, before releasing them to real-life. Hence, once the digital brain is created, it should be attached to the embodying service to learn from the service interactions.

To create digital brain as a service, every module in the Starzyk-Prasad model needs to be realized and encapsulated as a service. The high-level components will be added to the machine consciousness service such as the central executive unit and different memory units, while the low-level components will be added to the digital brain service such as the sensory and motor units, as seen in Table I. Hence, we need first to create encoder/decoder services, different memory services (i.e., episodic, semantic, and procedural), sensory and motor services, monitoring service, sub-cortical and emotion management services, attention switching service, motivation management service, and planning service. Then, we need to compose the brain and machine consciousness services from these components. We believe choreography is the suitable coordination style for these components services, as central orchestration will degrade the overall performance and limits possibilities for parallelization. We summarize the approach realization as follows:

- For building decoders/encoders services, different sparse encoders should be adopted for each data type such as the ones discussed in [12]. Decoders/encoders services pass the data from sensory units to sensory processors, and the decoders will pass the data from the motor processors to the motor units.
- For building memory services, we propose to build the episodic memory service adopting the model proposed in [18], and the procedural memory service adopting the model proposed in [19] (which realizes the motor-skills component in the Starzyk-Prasad model). This is because these models represent the state of the art for modeling episodic and procedural memories. The work in [21] showed that HTM outperformed many of the well-known neural models, such as ELM, ESN and LSTM. Additionally, HTM requires little or no hyper-parameter tuning. HTM is very suitable for concept identification and predictions. Hence, we propose to build the semantic memory service using HTM to represent learnt concepts/beliefes. Then, we need to integrate such concepts/beliefes with the pain-network to be able to learn the action suitable for every learnt concept/belief.
- For building the motivation service, we propose to adopt the motivation model of the the Starzyk-Prasad model [22], in which motivation is modelled via a pain network (i.e., connections between different sets of sensory, pains, biases, and actions neurons). The pain-network model is always changing according to the responses of different actions. We also propose to use ML as the digital brain action selection approach [15] because ML compromises between making gains and relieving pains using the pain network model. ML extends the well-known reinforcement learning approach, and use it when curiosity-based learning is needed. A current goal is selected based on a dominant pain signal, and it represents an intended action that the agent wants to perform.
- For building the planning and thinking service, we propose to use the attention switching approach proposed in [22] that is based on mental saccade mechanism. A "mental saccade is a concept created to mimic the well-established concept of "visual saccade [22]. The mental saccade identifies the object with the most salient features from all the collected information and makes it the attention spotlight. Then, it retrieves all

TABLE I. THE ROADMAP FOR REALIZING THE PROPOSED APPROACH

Implementing Service	Component	Realizing Solution
Digital Brain Service	Decoders/Encoders Services	Adopt different sparse encoders for each data type such as the ones discussed in [12].
	Sensory Processing Service	Handle the reflexive actions (retrieved from semantic and procedural memories).
	Motor Processing service	Execute action plans over different motor units (i.e., straightforward operations calls).
Machine Consciousness Service	Episodic Memory Service	Adopt the most recent model proposed in [18].
	Procedural Memory Service	Adopt the well-known model proposed in [19].
	Semantic Memory Service	Integrate the cortical earning algorithm (CLA) of HTM model [21] with the pain network model [15].
	Sub-Cortical Service	Adopting the pain-network and ML mechanism proposed in [15].
	Action Monitoring Service	Compare between predicted and actual actions' resposnes.
	Central Executive Service	Adopt the mental saccade, attention switching, and cognition techniques discussed in [22].

the corresponding information about this object to start the cognition and identification processes. This is done by adopting the well-established concept of a global workspace (summarized in [7]), where all the information of the activated processes are collected in one global space (i.e., an associative memory). This space is known as the "mental workplace. The operation of searching this mental workspace is known as a "mental saccade. Once the perceived input activates an object in the mental workspace, its corresponding information in the episodic memory and semantic memory are activated and uploaded to the mental workspace. Such updated mental workspace will be researched for a new mental saccade. The mental saccade mechanism adopts a simple winner-take-all approach to choose the attention spotlight among competing signals. A successful execution of a given action triggers the memorization of the discovered solution in the procedural memory, which in turn train itself to remember the best performing actions. This is needed to create rhythmic actions to avoid future planning for the same situations appeared before [15].

Table I indicates the major components of the machine consciousness model, and their proposed realizing solutions. It also shows the suggested implementing service for every component. This table provides the roadmap for building organic web services. By realizing the components indicated in this table, we can easily build the digital brain and the machine consciousness services from those components, as shown in the use case discussed in Section V.

V. A Use Case

This sections shows how the proposed approach could be adopted in real-life, and discusses a corresponding use case.

In our previous work in [3], we proposed the CRESCENT framework for managing composite web services. CRESCENT aimed to be autonomous, so it is designed to be self-healing, self-optimizing, and self-organizing. Therefore, it has modules for SLA management, workflow management, adaptive composition, capacity planning management, components provisioning, components discovery, dispatchers and monitors. Figure 3 depicts the main modules of the CRESCENT framework and their interactions. Unfortunately, CRESCENT is designed based on pre-defined rules and policies for detecting and replacing bad performing components. Hence, CRESCENT can ensure the managed composite web service to be autonomous, but not organic.

Given that we have a composite web service that realizes a given real-life business process, and we want to make this composite web service organic using the proposed approach, the CRESCENT framework should be extended to to create the digital brain service. This should be done by adding all the low-level components of the machine consciousness model (shown in Table I) to CRESCENT, where the other CRESCENT modules appear as different functional units in the digital brain service. Then, we need to create the machine consciousness service, which will have all high-level components of the machine consciousness model. Once the digital brain and the machine consciousness services are created, we connect the composite web service to be managed into the digital brain service, as in Figure 1. Then, we start the training process until all neural models converge. Finally, we release the digital brain and machine consciousness services to manage the composite web service in real-life situations, and let them grow and evolve.

VI. Conclusion and Future Work

This paper argued that to be able to build self-managing services, services are needed to be autonomic and organic. Therefore, this paper proposed a novel approach for building organic web services, in which a digital brain service is created to transform any ordinary service into an organic service. This is done by connecting the ordinary service to the digital brain service, which in turn is connected into a machine consciousness service to accomplish all cognition, thinking, learning, planning, and decision making tasks. The paper proposed to adopt the Starzyk-Prasad machine consciousness model to build both the digital brain and machine consciousness services, showing the mapping between the model's modules and the implementing services. The paper also discussed different problems that create obstacles for building the digital brain service (i.e., the representation problem, the memory modeling problem, the planning and thinking problem, and the motivation and learning problem), then it proposed solutions for every problem, creating a roadmap for building digital brains for software systems.

Future work will focus on implementing a prototype for the digital brain service, then training different instances of the digital brain service for different application domain business services. We believe extending the CRESCENT framework to include machine consciousness components is the way forward to build a digital brain prototype.

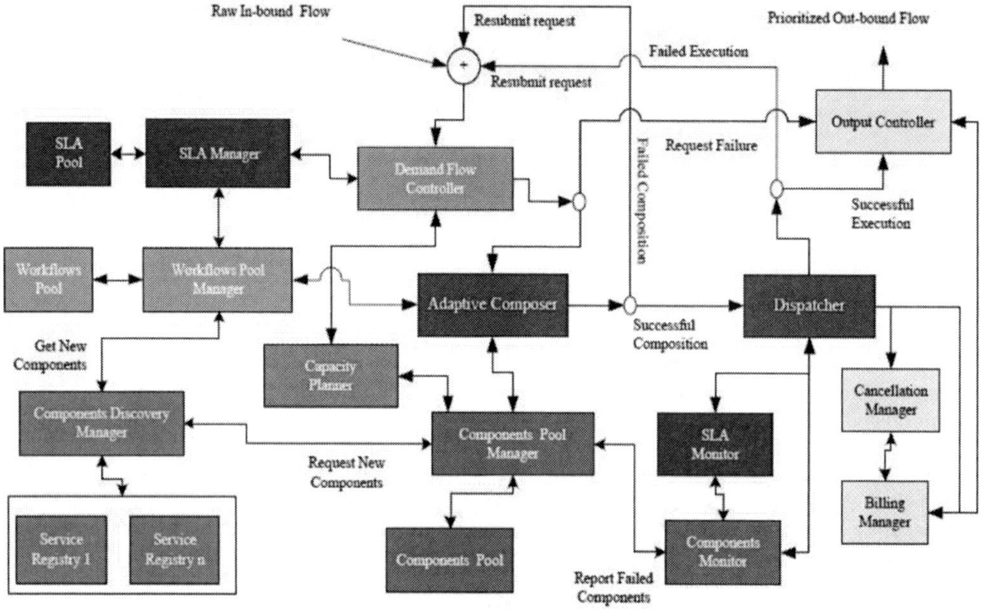

Figure 3. CRESCENT Architecture [3]

REFERENCES

[1] C. Müller-Schloer, "Organic computing: On the feasibility of controlled emergence," in Proceedings of the 2nd IEEE/ACM/IFIP International Conference on Hardware/Software Codesign and System Synthesis, 2004, pp. 2–5.

[2] J. O. Kephart and D. M. Chess, "The vision of autonomic computing," Computer, vol. 36, no. 1, Jan 2003, pp. 41–50.

[3] I. Elgedawy, "CRESCENT: A reliable framework for durable composite web services management," Computer Journal, vol. 58, no. 2, Feburary 2015, pp. 280–299.

[4] A. Lam, J. J. Q. Yu, Y. Hou, and V. O. K. Li, "Coordinated autonomous vehicle parking for vehicle-to-grid services: Formulation and distributed algorithm," IEEE Transactions on Smart Grid, vol. PP, no. 99, 2017, pp. 1–1.

[5] S. Singh and I. Chana, "Qos-aware autonomic resource management in cloud computing: A systematic review," ACM Comput. Surv., vol. 48, no. 3, Dec. 2015, pp. 42:1–42:46.

[6] D. Gamez, "Progress in machine consciousness," Consciousness and Cognition, vol. 17, no. 3, 2008, pp. 887 – 910.

[7] J. A. Reggia, "The rise of machine consciousness: Studying consciousness with computational models," Neural Networks, vol. 44, 2013, pp. 112 - 131.

[8] J. A. Starzyk and D. K. Prasad, "A computational model of machine consciousness," International Journal of Machine Consciousness, vol. 03, no. 02, 2011, pp. 255–281.

[9] I. Elgedawy, "Machine consciousness as a service (MCaaS): a roadmap," to appear, Iran Journal of Computer Science, Oct 2017.

[10] A. Chella and R. Manzotti, "Machine consciousness: A manifesto for robotics," International Journal of Machine Consciousness, vol. 01, no. 01, 2009, pp. 33–51.

[11] S. Ahmad and J. Hawkins, "Properties of sparse distributed representations and their application to hierarchical temporal memory," CoRR, vol. abs/1503.07469, 2015.

[12] K. Gupta and A. Majumdar, "Sparsely connected autoencoder," 2016 International Joint Conference on Neural Networks (IJCNN), 2016, pp. 1940–1947.

[13] S. Purdy, "Encoding data for htm systems," CoRR, vol. abs/1602.05925, 2016.

[14] T. T. Rogers and J. L. McClelland, "Prcis of semantic cognition: A parallel distributed processing approach," Behavioral and Brain Sciences, vol. 31, no. 6, 2008, p. 689714.

[15] J. A. Starzyk, J. T. Graham, P. Raif, and A.-H. Tan, "Motivated learning for the development of autonomous systems," Cognitive Systems Research, vol. 14, no. 1, 2012, pp. 10 – 25.

[16] J. Hawkins and D. George, "Hierarchical temporal memory concepts, theory, and terminology," in Technical report, Numenta, 2006.

[17] J. Hawkins, D. George, and J. Niemasik, "Sequence memory for prediction, inference and behaviour." Philosophical transactions of the Royal Society of London. Series B, Biological sciences, vol. 364 1521, 2009, pp. 1203–9.

[18] W. Wang, B. Subagdja, A. H. Tan, and J. A. Starzyk, "Neural modeling of episodic memory: Encoding, retrieval, and forgetting," IEEE Transactions on Neural Networks and Learning Systems, vol. 23, no. 10, Oct 2012, pp. 1574–1586.

[19] F. P. Tamborello, "A computational model of routine procedural memory," Ph.D. dissertation, 2009. [Online]. Available: https://search.proquest.com/docview/304989696?accountid=13014, [retrieved: 12, 2017]

[20] J. Graham, J. A. Starzyk, Z. Ni, H. He, T. H. Teng, and A. H. Tan, "A comparative study between motivated learning and reinforcement learning," in 2015 International Joint Conference on Neural Networks (IJCNN), July 2015, pp. 1–8.

[21] Y. Cui, C. Surpur, S. Ahmad, and J. Hawkins, "A comparative study of htm and other neural network models for online sequence learning with streaming data," 2016 International Joint Conference on Neural Networks (IJCNN), 2016, pp. 1530–1538.

[22] J. A. Starzyk, "Mental saccades in control of cognitive process," in The 2011 International Joint Conference on Neural Networks, 2011, pp. 495–502.

Handling Matrix Calculations with Microservices within Scenarios of Modern Mobility

Malte Zuch, Andreas Hausotter, Arne Koschel
University of Applied Sciences & Arts Hannover
Faculty IV, Department of Computer Science,
Hannover, Germany
email: Malte.Zuch@hs-hannover.de

***Abstract*—In the context of modern mobility, topics such as smart-cities, Car2Car-Communication, extensive vehicle sensor-data, e-mobility and charging point management systems have to be considered. These topics of modern mobility often have in common that they are characterized by complex and extensive data situations. Vehicle position data, sensor data or vehicle communication data must be preprocessed, aggregated and analyzed. In many cases, the data is interdependent. For example, the vehicle position data of electric vehicles and surrounding charging points have a dependence on one another and characterize a competition situation between the vehicles. In the case of Car2Car-Communication, the positions of the vehicles must also be viewed in relation to each other. The data are dependent on each other and will influence the ability to establish a communication. This dependency can provoke very complex and large data situations, which can no longer be treated efficiently. With this work, a model is presented in order to be able to map such typical data situations with a strong dependency of the data among each other. Microservices can help reduce complexity.**

Keywords–e-mobility; microservices; matrix calulations; workload decomposition

I. Introduction

In the context of modern mobility, there are often m to n assignments. In the field of e-mobility, m-vehicles are often considered in relation to n-charging points. Or for the real-time parking optimization, m-vehicles have to be optimized in relation to n-parking lots. Particularly in Car2Car-Communication, large swarms of vehicles have to be considered, in order to be able to identify all possible interaction points.

The basic data model is expressed in m-x-n or m-x-m matrices. The data are thus represented as normal adjacency matrices. These matrices can provoke large and complex data situations. By matrix multiplication of such matrices, additional data can be calculated which can be used in the area of Car2Car-Communication. This is the motivation of this work and will be explained in more detail below.

A. Motivation

For the analysis and optimization of scenarios of Car2Car-Communication, it is necessary to capture the whole data situation at first. It must be determined which vehicles have a favorable distance to other vehicles, in order to establish a communication bridge to each other.

For example, in Fig. 1 the distance from vehicle A to C may be too large to communicate with each other (Situation 2). However, communication from A through B to C could be enabled via a vehicle B close enough to vehicle A and C (Situation 1). In order to identify such a possible communication jump (and also 'deeper' jumps over several vehicles in between), large matrix multiplications are required, which can demand a lot of memory and cpu time. The next Section explains what this work will contribute concerning this topic.

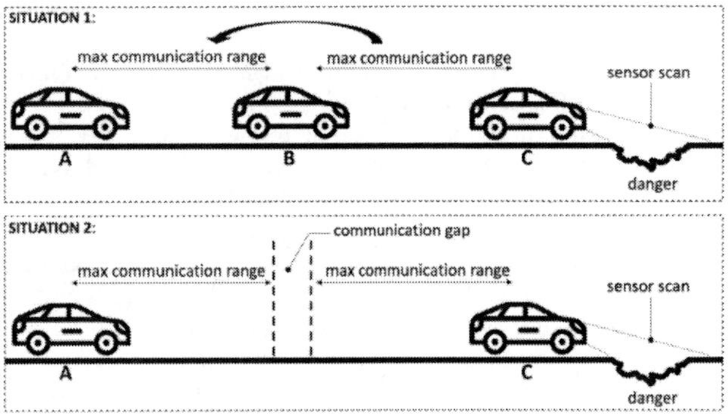

Figure 1. Situations of Car2Car-Communication

B. Contribution

The focus of this work is to deal with such large and deep matrix multiplications, which are often necessary within modern mobility scenarios and during the preparation of required data. These deep matrix multiplications can provoke a large demand for memory and cpu time and can exceed gives system capacities. Therefore, it is to be investigated how this large matrix multiplication problem can be treated more efficiently for applying of fine granular architecture concepts such as microservices. In this work, only the basic concept is presented, how calculation tasks of Car2Car scenarios can be decomposed. In the future, this decomposition could easily be implemented with microservices. In this work the mathematical model is explained and the microservices are only prototypically implemented in MATLAB [1] to illustrate the basic concept. For real applications, better runtime environments should be chosen. MATLAB was chosen only because it allows a very efficient matrix modeling. At first, the related work on this subject is shown in the Section II. In Section III the general data concept is presented and how this could be treated by the use of microservices. Further on, Section IV shows a number of exemplary measurements and how the computation resource demands can be reduced with this concept. The final Section V will summarize the results obtained and give an outlook on future work. But firstly, the next Section presents the related work on this topic.

II. Prior and Related Work

A general concept for a coordination system for optimizing the charging decision of electric vehicles were given in [2]. It was noted that concepts with parallel data processing would be necessary in the future in order to reactively cope with the coordination requirements of one million electric vehicles in Germany. In this respect, matrix models can be helpful in order to be able to partition the resulting data volumes. This was show in a prior work [3]. On the basis of these matrix models, optimization methods can help to assist electric vehicles in the search for electric charging stations. In an other previous work, first simulation results could show that vehicles can be supported theoretically and mutual blockages on load columns can be reduced. First synthetic simulation results show that up to plus 59 % more vehicles could be coordinated to electric charging stations [4].

A detailed overview concerning related matrix computation is given in [5]. A more detailed explanation of parallel matrix computation of thinly populated sparse-matrixes is given in this [6] related work. These sparse matrices could be used to reduce the volume of data. However, this is not part of this work. Here, the decomposition concept for the application of microservices will be presented. But these sparse matrix representations could help to understand modern matrix models and how they could be parallelized with regard to microservices. A general survey to microservices is presented in [7] and gives an overview of modern companies like Uber, Netflix, Amazon and Twitter using microservices.

The transition from monolithic application to modern microservices is shown in [8][9]. Both works give a good overview on the scaling of micro-services. This could be used in order to solve also large data problems, which among other things in the matrix models of this work are considered.

A recent survey of more than 100 IT companies has shown that only 20 % of companies are not considering microservices in their company decisions. For 80 % of the companies surveyed, microservices are already integrated or are currently in the integration process [10]. A similar survey confirms these findings, with 23.9 % of companies not yet in contact with microservices and the majority with 76.1 % are already in use of practicing or implementing microservices [11].

After this overview of the prior and related work, the general adjacency matrix model will be explained in the following Section.

III. THE CONCEPT FOR HANDLING HUGE MATRICES

This section deals with the core content. This is divided into two Sections. In Section III-A, fundamental matrix multiplications are addressed and how they are needed in modern mobility scenarios in order to be able to calculate dependencies and grouping dynamics of vehicle fleets. After the general calculation problem has been explained, Section III-B shows how this problem can be partitioned.

Large matrix multiplication often requires a lot of computing power. A linear increase in the number of columns and rows often results in a quadratic increase in the elements that must be calculated. Therefore, it makes sense to solve the problem from a certain problem size in sub-problems. These sub-problems can be solved, for example, with the concept of microservices. The general problem of those matrix multiplication in modern mobility scenarios is described in the following Section.

A. *The definition of the general calculation problem*

In many modern mobility scenarios, it is necessary to determine which vehicles have a small distance from each other and can form a local group. This is required, for example, in intelligent parking management system.

The larger the amount of vehicles in the same area, the harder the situation of competitive in finding free parking lots. Matrix multiplications of the adjacency matrix which contains the vehicle distances can be used to calculate where particularly strong competition situations occur. Car2Car-Communication especially is a even bigger problem. If it is to be calculated in real-time, which vehicles are currently close enough to form a cluster of Car2Car-Communications, this requires multiple matrix multiplications. So, in general, these multiple matrix multiplications are required in different modern mobility scenarios such as Car2Car-Communication or intelligent parking systems. Only for the example of Germany with about 45.8 million vehicles [12], this results in a large matrix multiplication with 48.5 million x 48.5 million entries.

Matrix multiplications can thus be used to determine, which vehicles can form a communication cluster together. This information can, for example, be used to initially exchange and aggregate sensor data among the vehicles in the cluster. Then, only a single vehicle provides all aggregated data via cellular connection to other clusters. This allows not all vehicles to communicate redundant information, but the information is only reported once per cluster. This can save bandwidth and relieve communication networks, especially if in the future millions of vehicles can send huge data in real-time. This scenario is shown in Fig. 2:

In order to identify dynamic clusters with matrix multiplications, a quadratic m-x-m matrix M is initially created in the dimension of the amount of m-vehicles. As soon as vehicles are below a maximum allowed communication distance r_{max} between each other, the matrix M receives a 1-entry. If vehicles are spaced apart from this distance, a 0-entry is made. This marks all vehicles that are too far apart to communicate directly with each other. Fig. 3 shows this:

This simple adjacency matrix M thus shows only the direct connections. As vehicle A is in communication range to B and B to C. D is not in range to any vehicle. But it is not directly apparent that an indirect connection of A over B to C is possible. This can be determined with matrix multiplications of the quadratic adjacency matrix M, containing the connections between the vehicles. The variable n describes the 'jump depth'. For example, for n = 2 it is possible to check whether vehicle A is indirectly connected to C via B.

$$Z_{tmp} = \sum_{i=1}^{n} M^i \tag{1}$$

As soon as an entry in Z_{tmp} is greater than 1, exactly 1 is entered at the same position in Z. Otherwise it is entered value 0:

$$Z_{i,j} = 1 \ if \ Z_{tmp_{i,j}} > 0 \tag{2}$$
$$Z_{i,j} = 0 \ if \ Z_{tmp_{i,j}} = 0 \tag{3}$$
$$for \ all \ i,j = [1, ..., m] \tag{4}$$
$$m: \ amount \ of \ vehicles \tag{5}$$

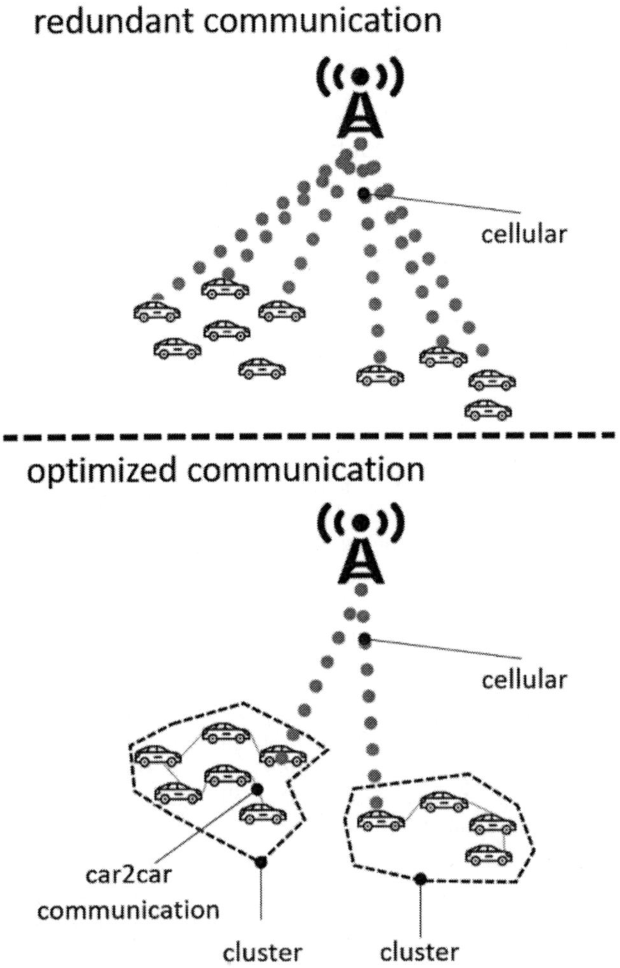

Figure 2. Scenario of Car2Car-Communication

The result of those calculation from M over Z_{tmp} to the final cluster-matrix Z is shown in Fig. 4. In this example, only $n = 3$ 'jumps' were calculated. So, it was calculated how indirect jumps over other vehicles will lead to a cluster connection.

Fig. 4 shows, that there is no connection for D to any other vehicle. But it shows, that there is a indirect connection between A and C. This information was not directly available in the primary matrix M. This new information in Z can now be used to optimize scenarios such as in Fig. 2.

With very large matrices, a very bulky and big problem arises. For the calculation of scenarios that take into account the entire German vehicle market, this would quickly lead to a large demand for computing power. In this regard, the next Section explains how this problem can be decomposed in order to solve it more efficiently in parallel (for example, with the future use of microservices).

B. The decomposition of the problem

For a simple matrix multiplication of 4x4 adjacency matrix $M_{tmp} = M*M$, many intermediate steps must be performed.

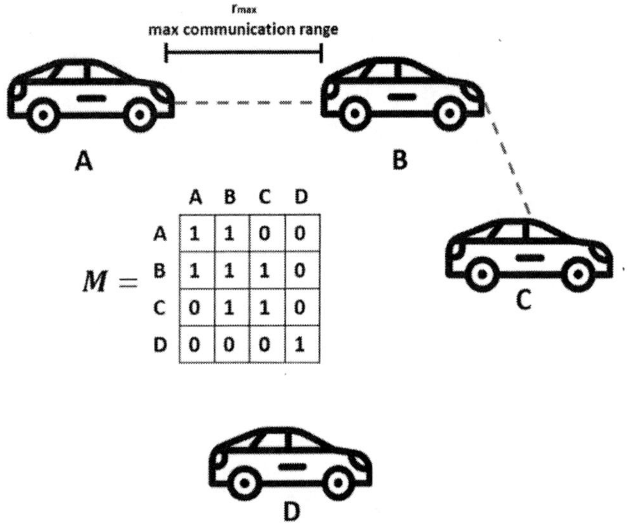

Figure 3. The primary distance matrix

For example, to calculate the element $M_{tmp_{1,2}}$, the following sub-calculations are needed:

$$M_{tmp_{1,2}} = M_{1,2}*M_{2,1}+M_{2,2}*M_{2,2}+M_{3,2}*M_{2,3}+M_{4,2}*M_{2,4} \quad (6)$$

In the case of very large matrices, the entire calculation effort should then be decomposed. Fig. 5 shows this exemplary.

A slightly more visual representation is provided in Fig. 6. This shows how parts of the original matrix can be broken down into different tasks.

For example, the two tasks, TASK_A and TASK_B could very easily be represented as microservice, as shown in Fig. 5. Particularly in the case of very large matrices, thousands of micoservices can solve the cluster building problem in parallel. Each microservice only needs a fraction of the system resources that would be required for the entire problem. The mathematical modeling presented here thus makes it possible to easily map the entire (huge) computing problem for small microservices.

In the next Section, this concept will be examined. Some measurements are made, in which the cpu time demand is documented. It will show how the decomposition of the general calculation problem in smaller sub-problems can help to save computing resources.

IV. Measuring the Effects

At first, the computing resources (CPU Time) for solving the total and undivided matrix multiplication is measured. The matrix has the dimension 1024 x 1024 and the depth of computation was $n = 3$ (see (1) and Fig. 4). It is therefore calculated which vehicles (indirectly) can build a Car2Car-Communication with each other. Indirect means that vehicles build a communication bridge over other vehicles that are close enough together in the cluster. Such a communication bridge over other vehicles is indicated in Fig. 3. For purposes of better illustration, only one communications bridge over a single vehicle is illustrated in Fig. 3. However, the following calculation considers communication bridges for a deeper

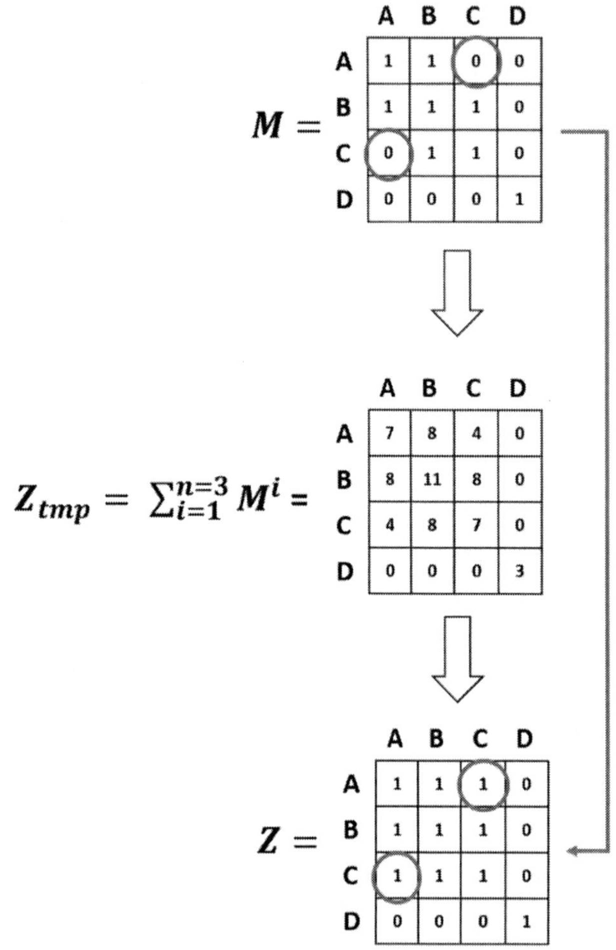

Figure 4. The result of the matrix multiplication

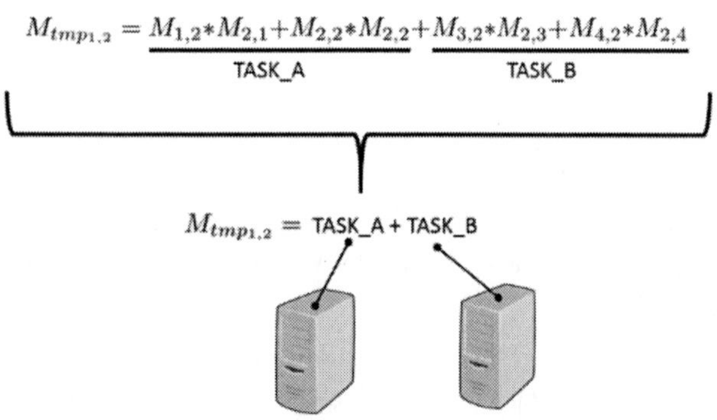

Figure 5. The decomposition of a matrix multiplication

calculation of a total of 3 vehicles. This is the calculation depth $n = 3$. The hardware corresponds to current standard hardware from the year 2017 with a 4x3.30 Ghz processor and 8 GB Ram.

Next, the problem is decomposed into several equal sub-problems as mentioned in Fig. 5. The parallel basic prototype

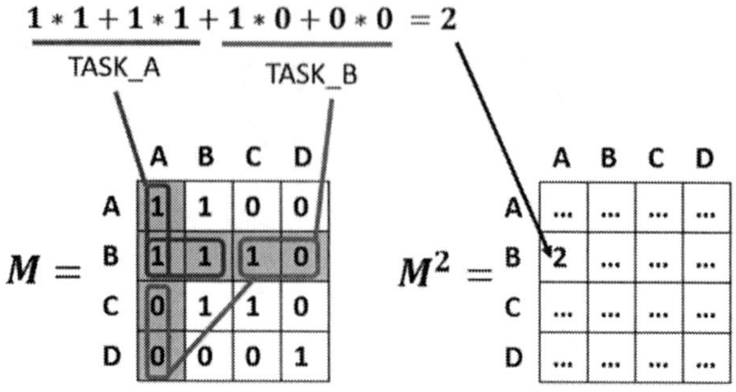

Figure 6. A example of matrix decomposition

microservices were realizes with MATLAB R2016b 64bit [1]. In future work, more common development environments and standards in designing microservices could be used [13] [14]. But for this first measurements of the general potential of partitioning, this more mathematical approach gives a quite good overview.

The dividing of a huge problem into smaller sub-problems reduces the general demand for computing resources per calculation instance, but also increases the communication overhead between all instances and will lead to a slightly longer time to calculate the problem. Depending on the cost of the microservices, the problem size and requirements with regard to real-time calculation, an different partitioning of the problem situation can be useful.

Table I gives a first impression, how different partitioning tasks affect the demand of computing resources (CPU Time) and the communication overhead (Communication Time).

TABLE I. THE EFFECT OF DECOMPOSITION

Partitions	*CPU Time*	*Communication Time*	*Total Time*
1	70.41 sec	0.0 sec	**70.41 sec**
2	32.09 sec	1.37 sec	**33.47 sec**
4	16.29 sec	2.48 sec	**18.77 sec**
8	8.38 sec	4.55 sec	**12.93 sec**
16	4.53 sec	8.84 sec	**13.38 sec**
32	2.60 sec	17.97 sec	**20.58 sec**
64	1.64 sec	36.32 sec	**37.97 sec**
128	1.13 sec	69.72 sec	**70.86 sec**
256	0.85 sec	138.97 sec	**139.83 sec**

The results from Table I were visualized in Fig. 7. It can be seen that a very high parallelization does not necessarily have to lead to a faster calculation.

It can be seen that with higher partitioning, the computation time per task decreases, but the communication effort to compose the final solution increases continually. With the used hardware (4x3.30 Ghz CPU and 8 GB Ram) the problem could be calculated fastest, if it is divided into eight sub-problems for the parallel calculation. This is marked in Fig. 7 with the dotted line. The optimal partitioning always depends on the hardware used. For the hardware used here, the optimum for partitioning is eight sub-problems. Cloud computing infrastructures with a large number of parallel processors would lead to even faster parallel calculations. But these first measurements can already show that a parallelization of matrix multiplications can lead to a efficient speed up.

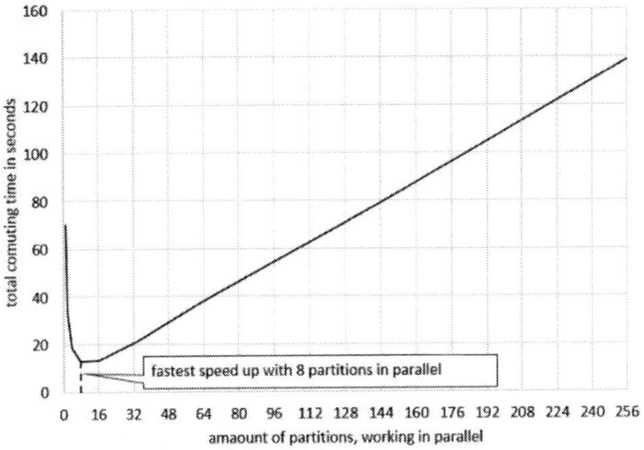

Figure 7. Visualization of the measurements

After presenting these first measurements, the next Section is followed by the discussion and outlook.

V. Conclusion

Without any partitioning, the total computing time was 70.41 sec. The best speed up was realized with a parallelization of 8, resulting in a total computing time of 12.93 sec. This is a speed up factor of 5.44x. A very fine partitioning with 256 partitions in parallel results in a total computing time of 138.83 sec. This is nearly two times slower than the initial computation time without any parallelization. So, the speed up factor was only 0.50x. This shows that the parallelization must be carefully chosen depending on the general size of the problem situation and the available hardware, in order to benefit from the optimal acceleration.

There are several parallelization possibilities. For example, the matrix multiplication could also be processed in parallel with typical MapReduce methods [15]. However, in the case of the MapReduce method, the coordination effort resulting from the map-layer and the reduction-layer, and the allocation to key-value pairs, can lead to somewhat more communication effort. But especially the matrix multiplications are characterized in particular by the fact that these can be split very easily. No prior sorting and assignment of the individual tasks to key-value pairs is necessary. The parallelization of matrix multiplication can be implemented very easily, without any key-value pairing and mapping-assignments (shown in Fig. 5). Therefore, the decomposition of huge matrix multiplication in very simple microservices seems to be appropriate.

Depending on the available computing power per microservice and the size of the overall problem, there is an optimum for the parallelization. With regard to the problems discussed here, it has been shown that the optimum of parallelization and additional communication effort is the fastest with a partitioning of 8 parallel tasks. Then the combination of additional communication effort and the acceleration of the parallelization is the fastest. With increasing parallelization, the pure calculation is still accelerated, but the entire processing time is reduced by the increasing communication effort, when the partial solutions are combined into the total solution.

In future work, the execution of the microservices with strongly optimized frameworks like Apache Hadoop / Spark [13] [14] could be investigated. The communication effort could be further reduced and even faster speed up factors could be reachable. So, summarizing, a parallelization of matrix multiplication (for example with the use of very simple microservices) can lead to a fast reduction in the computation time, but must be carefully chosen in order to achieve maximum efficiency.

References

[1] "The MathWorks, Inc." 2017, URL: https://mathworks.com/products/matlab.html [accessed: 2017-12-06].

[2] M. Zuch, A. Hausotter, and A. Koschel, "Efficiency in the electromobile mass market (Original German Title: Effizienz im elektromobilen Massenmarkt)," INFORMATIK 2015 – 45. Jahrestagung der Gesellschaft für Informatik, Cottbus (DE), vol. 45. Jahrestagung, 2015, pp. 5–6.

[3] M. Zuch, A. Koschel, and A. Hausotter, "Partitioning model for mobile electric vehicle data," Digital Marketplaces Unleashed - Mobility Services, vol. IEEE 2016, 2017, pp. 1–3.

[4] C. Linnhoff-Popien, R. Schneider, and M. Zaddach, Eds., Digital Marketplaces Unleashed. Springer, Berlin, Oct. 2017, ISBN: 978-3-662-49274-1.

[5] H. G. Gene and C. F. v. L., Eds., Digital Marketplaces Unleashed. J. Hopkins Uni. Press, Dec. 2012, ISBN: 978-1421407944.

[6] J. P. Gray, Ed., Parallel Computing: Technology and Practice. IOS Press, Apr. 1995, ISBN: 978-9051991963.

[7] R. RV, Ed., Spring Microservices. Packt Publishing, Birmingham, Jun. 2016, ISBN: 978-1786466686.

[8] S. Sharman, R. Rv, and G. D., Eds., Microservices: Building Scalable Software. Packt Publishing, Birmingham, Jan. 2017, ISBN: 978-1-78728-583-5.

[9] T. Hunter, Ed., Advanced Microservices: A Hands-on Approach to Microservice Infrastructure and Tooling. Apress, Jun. 2017, ISBN: 978-1484228869.

[10] "LeanIX Microservices Survey," 2017, URL: https://www.cio.de/a/microservices-machen-die-it-schneller-und-agiler,3329517 [accessed: 2017-12-06].

[11] "Microservices trends 2017: Strategies, tools and frameworks," 2017, URL: https://jaxenter.com/microservices-trends-2017-survey-133265.html [accessed: 2017-12-06].

[12] "Number of German passenger cars," 2017, URL: https://www.kba.de/DE/Statistik/Fahrzeuge/Bestand/bestand_node.html [accessed: 2017-12-06].

[13] "Apache Hadoop 2.7.4," 2017, URL: http://hadoop.apache.org/docs/stable/ [accessed: 2017-12-06].

[14] "Spark Overview," 2017, URL: https://spark.apache.org/docs/latest/ [accessed: 2017-12-06].

[15] J. Dean and S. Ghemawat, "MapReduce: Simplified Data Processing on Large Clusters," OSDI 2004, vol. Google Inc, 2004, pp. 2,4,10.

On Microservices in Smart Grid Capable pmCHP

Richard Pump
Arne Koschel
Volker Ahlers
Department of Computer Science
University of Applied Sciences and Arts
Hannover, Germany
Email: {richard.pump, arne.koschel, volker.ahlers}@hs-hannover.de

***Abstract*—Portable-micro-Combined-Heat-and-Power-units are a gateway technology bridging conventional vehicles and Battery Electric Vehicles (BEV). Being a new technology, new software has to be created that can be easily adapted to changing requirements. We propose and evaluate three different architectures based on three architectural paradigms. Using a scenario-based evaluation, we conclude that a Service-Oriented Architecture (SOA) using microservices provides a higher quality solution than a layered or Event-Driven Complex-Event-Processing (ED-CEP) approach. Future work will include implementation and simulation-driven evaluation.**

Keywords–Smart Grid; pmCHP; microservices; service-orientation.

I. INTRODUCTION

The energy grid of the future requires extremely interconnected devices to regulate the amount of energy produced precisely to the needed amounts. Former tree-like distribution networks are replaced with small autonomous microgrids which imitate a peer-to-peer network [1]. To coordinate a higher amount of generators, each device has to be intelligent.

Not only the energy grid is changing, also the automotive industry is in turmoil. More and more countries work on reducing the carbon footprint and greenhouse gases to fight climate change. Driven by legislation and public conscience the amount of BEVs is rising. However, low range and comfort (in comparison to conventional vehicles) keep consumers away.

Combining stationary small scale generation and mobile usage, the *University of Applied Sciences and Arts Hannover* is working on pmCHP. The pmCHP generates heat and electricity at much higher efficiency than comparable conventional devices. A novel feature of the pmCHP is the dual usage in buildings as well as BEV. In buildings, the pmCHP is attached to a smart grid and helps to cover peak loads, in a BEV the pmCHP enhances the passengers comfort and extends the range of the vehicle [2].

This contribution evaluates different software architectures for the control of the pmCHP, since the use in a constantly evolving Smart Grid requires a well-crafted adaptive Architecture. We will present three designs using different architectural paradigms and evaluate them using a scenario-based procedure. Section II will present related work, showing there is not much research concentrating on the architecture of pmCHP-Software. Section III presents the three developed architectures: SOA, ED-CEP, and layered. In Section IV and V, we evaluate the architectures using likely scenarios that the software will encounter over its lifespan. The last section concludes this work and gives some outlook to future work.

II. RELATED WORK

Regarding software-architectures for the smart grid, mostly interactions are standardized. For example, the Standards 61968/61970, designed by the International Electrotechnical Commission (IEC) describe a global domain model of the smart grid with pre-defined interfaces and messages. The Standards however do not describe a pre-defined internal software architecture.

In [3], Reinprecht et. al. describe the IEC Common Information Model (CIM) architecture, which is a layered architecture that ensures Standard compliant implementation over the different levels of the architecture. The authors describe multiple SOA-based designs which were created for the Smart Grid Interoperability test. A comparison or evaluation of the architectures is not mentioned.

Appelrath et. al. [4] show a reference architecture for smart grid software. It describes general interfaces for abstract devices, a real device might be composed of multiple abstract ones. However, neither a concrete implementation nor an evaluation of alternatives is presented.

An architecture to operate a pmCHP testbed is presented in [5]. There is no connection to the smart grid, although microservices are used to provide high architectural flexibility.

To compare different architectural designs, Kazman et. al. [6] present a scenario-driven comparison method that provides the general process used in this work.

The most important quality-aspects of smart grid software are proposed by the NIST in [7]. Since the Smart Grid is critical infrastructure one of the most desired qualities is the availability of the devices. These qualities are considered when comparing the different designs in section IV.

All considered there is no concrete work on how to integrate a pmCHP into a smart grid, let alone an evaluation of suitable software architectures for this purpose, known to the authors of this paper.

III. ARCHITECTURES

To compare different architectures, a rough sketch of the desired components is needed, ensuring functional and conceptual similarity. The goal of the software is to drive the pmCHP according to different energy requests with regards to the operational strategy. Energy requests can be accepted from an external source, like the smart grid or originate from an internal source. The requests arriving at the software have to be incorporated into the current operational plan, which defines the pmCHPs operation.

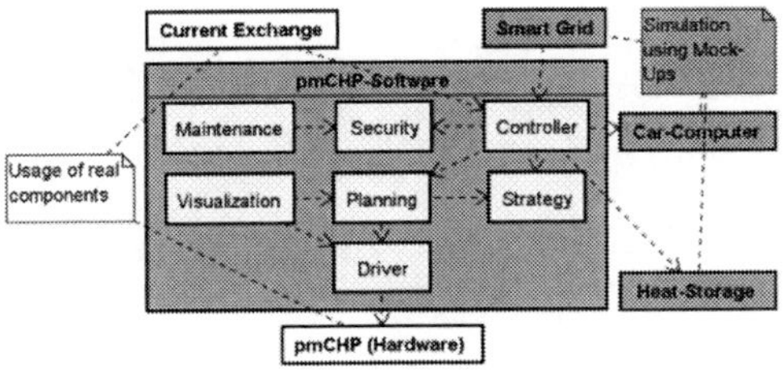

Figure 1. Rough sketch of the pmCHP-Software

Figure 1 shows the principal components of the pmCHP software.

The CONTROLLER coordinates the production of the pmCHP with its environment, be it the Smart Grid or the computer of the BEV. It receives energy requests, validates their security, and checks if they can be fulfilled. Valid requests are handed the PLANNING for further processing.

The component STRATEGY provides the framework for the day-planning, as it decides which operational strategy is used. The pmCHP can be used in three different modes; electricity-driven, heat-driven, and combined heat- and electricity-driven. The electrically-driven mode controls the production of the pmCHP depending on the needed electricity, heat is seen as byproduct and will not be produced if no electricity is needed. In heat-driven mode, the pmCHP uses the heating requirements as the control value, the combined operation mode just produces depending on whichever energy is needed at the time. STRATEGY has to decide which of the three modes is the most sensible, depending on the operating environment of the pmCHP.

The component PLANNING is responsible for planning the day-to-day-operation of the pmCHP, according to the operational strategy. It uses data about previous operation and forecasts to create an operational plan which is used by the DRIVER to control the pmCHP. The Component DRIVER transforms the operational plan into control-commands, monitors the pmCHP state, and provides this information to other parts of the software.

The VISUALIZATION component presents the current state and planned operation to the user of the device. Also errors and warnings can be shown to the user, so corrective action can be taken if needed.

To facilitate remote access to the pmCHP in case the software needs to be updated or other remote action needs to be taken, the component MAINTENANCE exists. It allows remote software updates, access to log files and current operational status of the pmCHP as well as remote control in case the grid operating company needs to control the pmCHP manually.

Allowing remote access to the pmCHP Software without any security measures would be grossly negligent, therefore a component SECURITY needs to take care of authentication and authorization of all incoming requests.

Other Components like SMART GRID, CURRENT EXCHANGE, etc. are beyond the scope of the software and represent neighboring systems to interact with.

Based on the previously shown rough design, three different architectural styles were used to create three architectures: SOA, ED-CEP and layered.

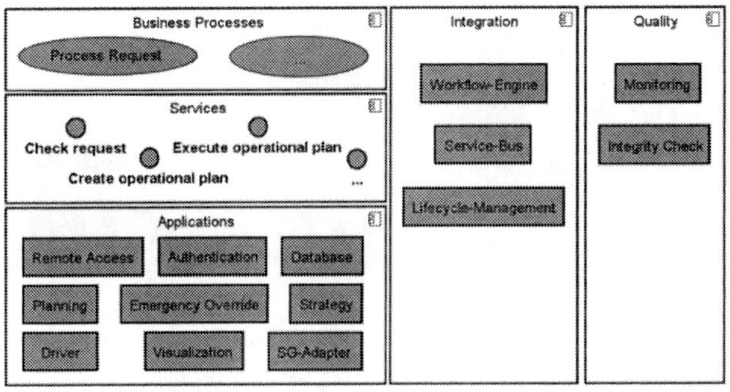

Figure 2. Overview of the SOA. (Not all services and processes are being shown to simplify presentation.)

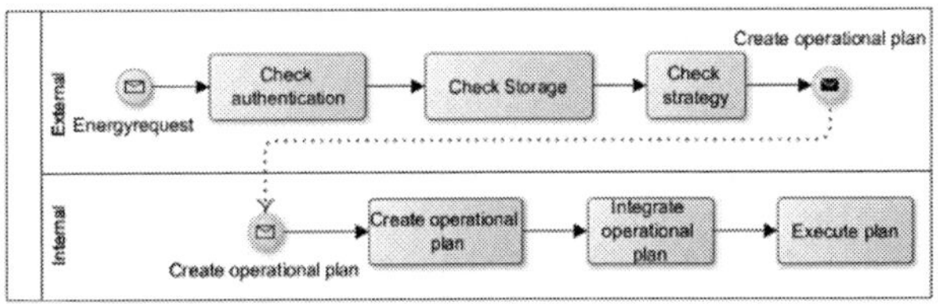

Figure 3. Business process: 'Process energy-request'.

A. *Service-oriented Architecture*

Service-oriented architectures use loose coupling and high cohesion in all parts of the software to achieve high flexibility under changing requirements [8]. They can be used in combination with microservices to allow for rapid redevelopment of all parts of the software.

In a SOA, the high level functions of the software are mapped to business processes which compose the services into useful processes. The services are responsible for small parts of functionality which can be reused in different contexts. Therefore, to create a service-oriented architecture for the pmCHP the usage scenarios need to be translated into business processes, which in turn need to be decomposed into small services, fit for a microservice approach.

Converting the rough sketch of Figure 1 into a SOA can result in the design shown in Figure 2. There are 13 business processes using over 20 different services, using the different Applications.

The most important business process is the processing of energy requests, arriving from an external source or created by the software itself, as shown in Figure 3. If a request arrives at the software at first the authenticity of the requests needs to be checked. If the request is valid, storage and strategy have to be checked; maybe the request can be fulfilled just by using the attached storage or cannot be fulfilled because of the currently selected operational strategy.

Assuming that a request is correct, another process is started, which creates an operational plan to fulfill the request, integrates that plan into the currently executed plan, and then executes the result using the driver. Requests not always originate from an external source, sometimes the software itself creates energy requests to achieve own interests. Internal requests do not need validation or crosschecking with storage

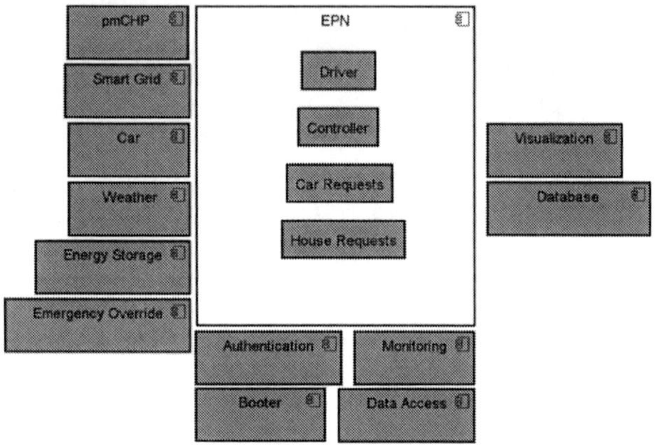

Figure 4. Components of the event-driven architecture.

and strategy.

The Services used in the process are rather simple and only take care of a single functionality. For example, the service 'Check request' simply checks the requests validity; i.e. through using a signature. The services are implemented in so called applications to keep similar functionalities under the same name; an application can contain one or multiple microservices. In general, there is no direct interaction between the services, for orchestration a workflow-engine is used, which translates the business processes into service-calls.

B. *Event-driven complex-event-processing*

An ED-CEP-architecture divides the software into two major parts. Main controlling logic and business processes central to the software are mapped to event-processor-chains in the Event-Processing-Network (EPN), while the surrounding applications provide services for tasks to be executed [9].

Figures 4 and 5 show the components of the architecture and the EPN, respectively. There is a notably similarity between the applications of the ED-CEP and the applications in the SOA, since the components fulfill similar roles in both architectural styles.

To ease comparison to the SOA, we will trace the events responsible to process an energy request from the smart grid in the EPN. With Figure 5 in mind, any smart grid requests enter the EPN through the SG-ADAPTER, which creates a *request*-event. *Request*-events in general are processed by the CONTROLLER, which after some processing creates an operational plan and wraps it in a *plan*-event. Using information from the *plan*-event the DRIVER creates *control*-events which are processed by the PMCHP to control the physical device. Further *notification*- and *operational data*-events are created, which are used to by different sinks.

C. *Layered approach*

The layered approach follows the simple principle, that components of a higher layer might use components of lower layers but not vice versa [10]. Generally, components will be divided into five layers, presentation/interface, requirements, business logic, technical logic, and data/hardware. Figure 6 gives an overview about the components of our layered architecture.

Figure 5. The Event-Processing-Network of the ED-CEP, showing Events and their flow from sources to sinks.

The *presentation/interface*-layer allows access to the functionalities of the software for external actors like other software and the user. Of note are the components EMERGENCY and MAINTENANCE, allowing other systems direct access to functions of the software.

Below the *Access*-layer are the three core logic layers of the software, decreasing in abstractness the further 'down' the architecture we traverse.

First is the *Request*-layer. Three different components make up the *Request*-layer, SMART GRID-REQUESTS, REQUESTCREATION CAR, and REQUESTCREATION BUILDING. While the first handles requests from the smart grid, the latter two create energy requests according to the operational strategy.

The second core layer is called the *Business Logic*, containing the components PLANNING and STRATEGY responsible for transforming the different requests into a single operational plan which can be executed by the lower layers.

Beneath, the third logic layer contains components which provide *technical* functionalities not dependent on external systems while being responsible for essential operations in the system. For example, the component BOOTER starts the whole system, initializing the other components.

The lowest layers *Data* and *Adapter* connect the software to other devices and systems, allowing operational data to be stored and queried, information about surrounding systems to be collected, and interaction with the pmCHP.

Figure 7 shows how the different components interact when a energy request arrives at the system. After being passed through to the AUTHENTICATION, the request is handled by the component SMART-GRID-REQUESTS where it is converted into an operational plan that can be executed by the DRIVER.

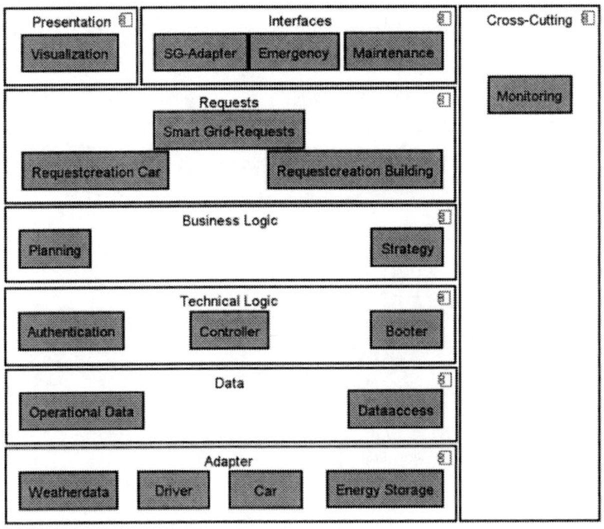

Figure 6. Decomposition of the components into layers following a canonical layered approach.

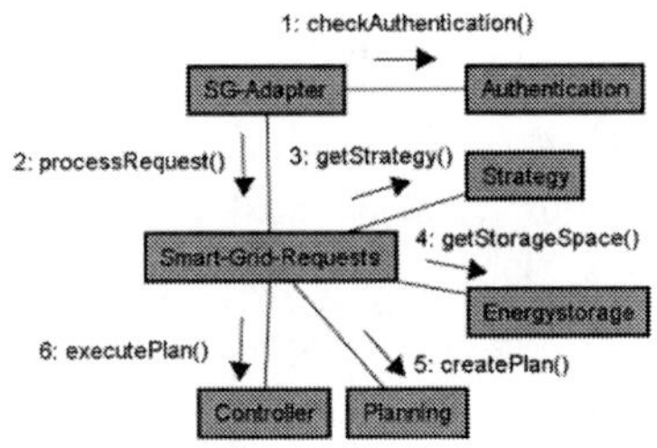

Figure 7. Interactions of the components required to process an energy request.

IV. COMPARISON OF ARCHITECTURES

Comparisons of architectures are a useful tool to increase software quality at an early stage of the development cycle [11]. Choosing the wrong architecture can decrease the maximum achievable quality by forcing bad design. For example, forcing an EPN into a micro-controller controlling a toaster will have less performance and increased development cost over a monolithic software. (Assuming the software is tasked with just turning the toaster off as soon as a signal is received. EPNs most likely handle complex scenarios better than monolithic approaches.)

Multiple ways exist to compare different architectures, but most commonly scenario-based methods are used. Scenario based methods use scenarios to estimate necessary changes to the architecture, which in turn can be used as an indicator for the quality of the architecture. The first step of a comparison is the definition of the architectures in some form, as already described in the previous section. In a second step, scenarios describing possible usages or changes of the architecture are defined, each providing a measurable way to describe quality. The scenarios are grouped after the five general aspects of software quality and use the rough system sketch as a common baseline for all architectures.

a) Availability: Availability scenarios describe situations in which the system has to take certain countermeasures to provide uninterrupted operation. Availability is the most important quality in an energy providing system [7].

Ava01 The DRIVER crashes due to an error, the system realizes the failure and immediately switches to a backup.

Ava02 The DRIVER receives a single incorrect measured value outside of the defined thresholds for this sensor. Instead of immediately shutting down the pmCHP the DRIVER averages values and prevents shutdown due to measurement errors.

Ava03 The connection between the DRIVER and the pmCHP is severed and cannot be reestablished. An error is presented to the user and the pmCHP switches to a safe operating mode instead of shutting down immediately.

Ava04 A usual high amount of energy requests is received from the smart grid. After a certain threshold is reached, the CONTROLLER rejects all further requests to provide protection against overload-attacks.

b) Security: Security-scenarios describe situations in which the software is possibly used in a way that it is not intended and unwanted. In an interconnected network with access to physical systems, security is one of the most important qualities the software has to achieve.

Sec01 A different system tries to access a pmCHP-software functionality, the authenticity of the accessing system is checked, before access is granted.

Sec02 When the pmCHP is activated, a minimal software checks the integrity of the pmCHP-software using a digital signature. If the signature is not correct, an error is presented to the user, and the software does not start.

Sec03 A manipulated component tries to access a function of the DRIVER which it normally would not access and is not authorized to do so. The component SECURITY recognizes the unauthorized attempt, prevents it and produces an error message shown to the user.

c) Safety: In contrast to security, safety-scenarios are describing potentially dangerous situations in the normal operation of the pmCHP-software. Again safety is rather important in operating an energy generating device, as failures can harm humans and the operating environment.

Saf01 The DRIVER continuously monitors all of the pmCHPs sensors and detects dangerous operation. If a dangerous operation is recognized, the DRIVER transfers the pmCHP into a safe mode of operations, possibly even shutting it down.

Saf02 All control-signals are checked by the DRIVER, ignoring signals that might damage the pmCHP.

d) Maintainability: Since the smart grid is not completely clear at the moment, adaptability and maintainability is somewhat needed. The following scenarios include likely changes and developmental processes of the software's lifetime.

Mai01 After the end of the pmCHP-development a different developer is tasked to add smart market integration to the pmCHP-software. The smart market component needs to accept requests from the smart grid, overview their execution, and take care of the billing aspects according to the energy contract.

Mai02 The emergency shutdown shall be tested intensively; the required components can be interchanged with mock-ups without changing the DRIVER.

Mai03 The systems architecture is checked by a software architect. Similar problems are solved in similar ways using similar architectural or design patterns.

e) Performance: Performance is not overall important to the pmCHP-software, only a single scenario is presented.

Per01 A malfunction of the pmCHP requires an emergency shutdown, the shutdown happens fast enough to prevent damage.

f) Usability: Usability describes the grade at which the user's interaction is eased by good interface and software design. Since there is almost no interaction of the user with the pmCHP-software, usability is an afterthought.

Usa01 To start or stop the pmCHP, only a single button has to be pressed by the user.

Usa02 After being started the software presents the momentary state of the pmCHP and can display the current operational planning.

A. Evaluation

To evaluate the architectures, we trace the necessary changes to the different architectures when applying the scenarios. We differentiate between easy changes, which will take some hours and difficult changes which will probably take significantly longer to execute. This provides an estimate for the loose coupling and functional adequateness of the architecture; if a functionality change incorporates changing a lot of components, loose coupling might not be present or the architecture might not have been designed with the scenario in mind and does not cover the requirements adequately.

For example, the scenario [Mai01] requires a new business process and a new service in the SOA, which equates in three changes to the architecture. To facilitate billing, the process to *process requests* has to be extended with service calls to a new service BILLING. Also the service bus has to be modified to connect the service to the application containing the logic.

The ED-CEP-architecture however requires a lot of changes, changing the REQUEST-event to accommodate the information necessary for the billing requires changes in all REQUEST-event-processing components. Also new events and processors for the billing itself have to be created.

Including the smart market into the layered architecture requires changes to two existing components and a new component; changing the SG-ADAPTER and the SMART GRID REQUEST to pass the needed data and oversee the completion of an order, as well as a new BILLING-adapter connecting to the appropriate smart market.

For brevity, we skip the evaluation of each architecture using every mentioned scenario and directly present the results.

TABLE I. COUNT OF CHANGES TO COMPONENTS NECESSARY TO FULFILL ALL SCENARIOS.

SOA Component	Count	ED-CEP Component	Count	Layers Component	Count
Driver (difficult)	2	Driver	3	Driver (difficult)	3
ServiceBus	2	SG-Adapter	2	SG-Adapter	2
WfE	1	Controller	2	Controller	1
process request	1	Driver (difficult)	1	Maintenance	1
Billing*	1	Planning	1	Visualization	1
		Emergency override	1	Smart Grid-request	1
		Monitoring	1	Billing	1
		Booter	1	Booter	1
		Request	1		
		Billing-event	1		
		Billing	1		
Total:	7		16		13
of total					
- difficult:	2		1		3
- easy:	5		15		10

B. Evaluation results

Table I shows the amount of changes necessary to the architectures. Overall, the event-driven complex-event-processing-architecture needs the most number of changes (although most of them easy), while the layered-architecture needs the most difficult changes.

The high number of changes to the ED-CEP-architecture originate from the scenario to integrate the software into the smart market, since a long chain of interactions had to be changed to facilitate billing. Also to isolate the DRIVERs functions from the rest of the architecture, checking access at every possible place, a lot of changes had to be made. Of note however is the ease with which changes (e.g. detection of dangerous operational states) can be done to the DRIVER of the CEP architecture. The rule-based implementation of logic provides an easy, powerful way to define actions on detection of certain states. In contrast, applying the same change to the service-oriented or the layered architecture requires more work to incorporate complex condition-action-mechanisms.

There are a lot of difficult changes which need to be applied to the layered architecture, mostly concerning the DRIVER. These primarily originate in the scenarios [Sec03], [Saf01], and [Saf02] each requiring a lot of functionality to be added to the component, since no other component is be responsible for the needed functions.

The SOA however requires the least amount of changes. Adding a smart market integration for example requires the least amount of changes in the SOA, while more extensive changes have to be made to the CEP or the layered architecture. The fine grained nature of the underlying microservices also helps the maintainability and flexibility of the software.

Assuming difficult changes need a lot more time than easy ones and a high amount of time needed is a sign of a bad architecture the following ranking can be created:

1) SOA using microservices
2) ED-CEP
3) Layered architecture

Considering this, we can infer that the SOA provides the loosest coupling and the highest functional adequateness for our scenario.

C. Scenario interactions

After checking loose coupling and functional adequateness, we need to validate the cohesion of the components, i.e. the proper separation of functionalities into components. Since every scenario should concern a single functionality, we can check the proper separation by looking for components which interact with more than one scenario.

Table II shows the components which are affected by multiple scenarios.

TABLE II. COUNT OF SCENARIO INTERACTIONS WHEN APPLYING THE SCENARIOS TO THE COMPONENTS OF THE DIFFERENT ARCHITECTURES.

SOA Component	Count	CEP Component	Count	Layers Component	Count
Driver	2	Driver	4	Driver	3
ServiceBus	2	SG-Adapter	2	SG-Adapter	2
		Planning	2		
		Controller	2		

Under this metric, the CEP-architecture is the worst of the three. The division of a functionality over a lot of small components (i.e. events) proves to be a negative factor under the scenario interaction. This infers an unclear separation of functionality over the components.

Layers and the SOA seem to be somewhat equal concerning scenario interaction, especially the driver seems to be a component which needs further refinement.

Under the scenario interaction metric, no clear ranking can be established, the layered approach and the SOA seem to be equal, the CEP seems to be the worst.

V. EVALUATION

Considering the previous sections, the SOA can be inferred to be the best choice for the integration of a pmCHP into the smart grid.

Especially the loose coupling and ease of change of service orientation and microservices help to create an architecture with a high grade of flexibility. In scenarios where a lot of changes to the other two architectures were necessary, SOA needed only a small amount of little changes. Considering the unclear future of the pmCHP-software this high flexibility is a very desirable property.

The layered architecture however is not a good choice, since it requires a relatively high amount of difficult changes to adapt to the scenarios, meaning more work in the long term. Similarly, the ED-CEP-architecture seems a bad fit for the problem. This however might be explained by insufficient design or bad evaluation-metrics. Counting the number of changes to introduce a new process into an EPN has to result in a high amount of changes, since a lot of small components need to be added, resulting in a bad score. If we look at the EPN as a whole however, only a single component changes in a lot of scenarios, interaction however grows also. A good way to handle this might be to split the EPN in smaller function-specific EPNs.

VI. CONCLUSION AND FUTURE WORK

We designed and evaluated three different designs to integrate pmCHP into a future smart grid. Using a scenario-based comparison we conclude that the usage of microservices can result in testable better architectures when a high degree of flexibility is needed. This is mostly due to the few interactions between Microservices in a SOA; a business process can just chain service-calls to achieve its desired result. To make changes to a certain functionality, services can be changed independently, new services can be introduced without changing others.

The results of this paper however only hold for the special case of integrating a pmCHP into a smart grid, other goals will likely result in different results.

Also, since all architectures have been developed by the same person over a short span of time, they likely influence each other. Especially the CEP and the SOA share some applications, which can also be explained by similar design philosophies. Further work combining the two might prove an even better solution for the smart grid integration of pmCHP.

In future steps, we will implement the SOA and evaluate the impact of pmCHPs in a smart grid.

ACKNOWLEDGMENT

This work was supported by the VolkswagenStiftung and the Ministry for Science and Culture of Lower Saxony (project funding number VWZN2891). We would like to thank all our colleagues from the research focus Scalability of mobile Micro-CHP units and the Institute for Engineering Design, Mechatronics and Electro Mobility (IKME) for their support and the productive cooperation.

REFERENCES

[1] H. Farhangi, "The path of the smart grid," Power and energy magazine, IEEE, vol. 8, no. 1, 2010, pp. 18–28.

[2] C. Schmicke, J. Minnrich, H. Rüscher, and L.-O. Gusig, "Development of range extenders to mobile micro combined heat and power units in vehicles and buildings; *Weiterentwicklung von Range Extendern zu mobilem mikro-Blockheizkraftwerken in Fahrzeugen und Gebäuden*," Techniktagung Kraft-Wärme-Kopplungssysteme, April 2014.

[3] N. Reinprecht, J. Torres, and M. Maia, "IEC CIM architecture for Smart Grid to achieve interoperability," International CIM Interop in March 2011, 2011.

[4] H.-J. Appelrath, L. Bischofs, P. Beenken, and M. Uslar, IT-architecture-development in the Smart Grid; *IT-Architekturentwicklung im Smart Grid*. Springer, 2012.

[5] C. Schmicke, J. Minnrich, H. Rüscher, and L.-O. Gusig, "Examination of mobile micro-chp on testbeds of the University of applied Sciences and Arts Hanover; *Untersuchung von mobilen mikro-BHKW an Prüfständen der Hochschule Hannover*," Ingenieurspiegel, vol. 4, 2015, pp. 60–61.

[6] R. Kazman, G. Abowd, L. Bass, and P. Clements, "Scenario-based analysis of software architecture," IEEE Software, vol. 13, no. 6, Nov 1996, pp. 47–55.

[7] A. Lee and T. Brewer, "Smart grid cyber security strategy and requirements," Draft Interagency Report NISTIR, vol. 7628, 2009.

[8] A. Arsanjani, "Service-oriented modeling and architecture," https://www.ibm.com/developerworks/library/ws-soa-design1/ 2017.11.01, November 2004.

[9] R. Bruns and J. Dunkel, Event-driven architectures: software architecture for event-driven business-processes; *Event-driven architecture: Softwarearchitektur für ereignisgesteuerte Geschäftsprozesse*. Springer-Verlag, 2010.

[10] E. W. Dijkstra, "Structure of an extendable operating system," http://www.cs.utexas.edu/users/EWD/ewd02xx/EWD275.PDF 2017.11.01, November 1969, circulated privately.

[11] P. Clements, R. Kazman, and M. Klein, Evaluating software architectures. Addison-Wesley Professional, 2003.

Teaching Microservices in the Private Cloud by Example of the eduDScloud

Dominik Schöner, Arne Koschel, Felix Heine

Faculty IV, Department of Computer Science
University of Applied Sciences and Arts
Hannover, Germany
Email: dominik.schoener@hs-hannover.de
Email: arne.koschel@hs-hannover.de
Email: felix.heine@hs-hannover.de

***Abstract*—Cloud computing has become well established in private and public sector projects over the past few years, opening ever new opportunities for research and development, but also for education. One of these opportunities presents itself in the form of dynamically deployable, virtual lab environments, granting educational institutions increased flexibility with the allocation of their computing resources. These fully sandboxed labs provide students with their own, internal network and full access to all machines within, granting them the flexibility necessary to gather hands-on experience with building heterogeneous microservice architectures. The eduDScloud provides a private cloud infrastructure to which labs like the microservice lab outlined in this paper can be flexibly deployed at a moment's notice.**

Keywords–education; private cloud; virtual lab; microservices; SOA; eduDScloud.

I. INTRODUCTION

After cloud computing in general and private cloud computing in particular crested the 'Peak of Inflated Expectations' in Gartner's 2010 Emerging Technologies Hype Cycle [1], the technology has become widely accepted by and used not only in the industry. But due to the versatility of its basic concepts, cloud computing not only offers opportunities for commercial, but for educational and research applications as well.

At institutions focussing on education and research, it is not uncommon that computing resources for use by individual students or groups are very limited, with most resources only being available in the form of shared, pre-installed environment, often used by multiple lectures at a time. While this essentially reduces cost for hardware and personnel, it also requires very restrictive permissions to be imposed on student accounts, in order to prevent users from affecting each other, effectively limiting the possibilities for exercises and projects.

When teaching microservices meanwhile, granting students administrative access to certain systems can be essential in allowing them to gather first-hand experience on the effects of changes to system and network configuration. For scenarios like these, cloud computing can offer a way to provide labs individual, virtual machines (VMs) and networking in sandboxed environments on dynamically assignable and expandable resources, which can easily be repurposed between lectures or labs.

An example of this is the eduDScloud (*edu*cational *d*ata analytics and *s*ervice-oriented architecture *cloud*), which is used at the University of Applied Sciences and Arts Hannover in lectures and labs on data analytics and distributed systems. This paper describes the architecture of the eduDScloud using the example of a virtual lab developed for teaching service-oriented and especially microservice architectures.

The remainder of this paper is structured as follows: Section II summarises related research followed by an overview of the requirements posed by a microservice lab scenario in Section III. The system's architecture is described in Section IV, with Section V detailing the setup of the microservice lab itself and the technologies used therein. In Section VI, the findings of this paper are then summarised, before an outlook on future research is given in Section VII.

II. RELATED WORK

The scenarios in which institutions make use of cloud computing in their educational programmes are becoming ever more diverse. Ranging from generic, collaborative Software-as-a-Service (SaaS) platforms like Google's G Suite for Education [2], to specialised platforms, e.g., for teaching high-performance computing [3] or R and Scilab [4].

Other platforms like CloudIA, proposed in [5], offer a combination of SaaS, Platform-as-a-Service (PaaS) and Infrastructure-as-a-Service in a single system, capable of running in a hybrid cloud context, scaling out to Amazon Web Services as needed. Their focus in PaaS lies within the on-demand deployment of individual VMs using a self-service portal accessible by students and lecturers. But without the concept of combining them into labs with customised, internal networking, it is impractical to use for the purpose of setting up a fully featured microservices lab.

III. REQUIREMENTS

To reach the goal of providing students with a virtual hands-on lab for exploring both classic service-oriented, as well as microservice architectures a number of requirements (labelled RQ1 through RQ8 for easier reference) must be met by different parts of the overall system. While many of these are imposed by the services scenario itself, some also originate from the infrastructure surrounding the cloud itself.

Although there is no single, agreed upon, complete definition of the term microservice, many authors agree that the autonomy and technology heterogeneity of microservices is a key requirement to providing lose coupling and ease of deployment [6] [7]. Offering these two characteristics in a lab requires it to run multiple machines (RQ1) to which students have full root access (RQ2), allowing them to either install

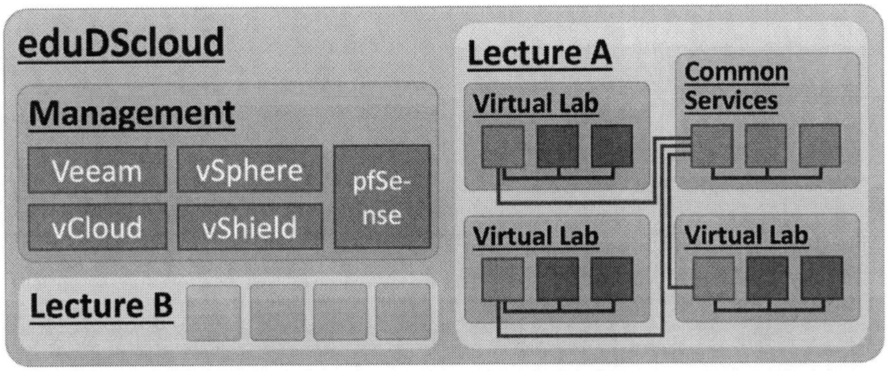

Figure 1. Schematic overview of the eduDScloud's overall architecture, detailing the connectivity between individual virtual labs (blue) and common services (green) within a lecture. The pfSense nodes (orange) can optionally also act as gateways to the internet or other internal networks.

arbitrary components or deploy containers (e.g., Docker) for individual microservices.

When providing users with extensive privileges like the aforementioned root level access, it is crucial to keep each virtual lab instance from adversely affecting others (RQ3), while still enabling full network access between its machines, as well as those of the students (RQ4). Additionally, it should be possible to create limited connectivity between individual labs for integration exercises (RQ5) and reset a lab instance in case of fatal misconfiguration (RQ6).

Since the focus of the microservices lab is on teaching service-oriented architecture (SOA) in general and microservice architectures in specific, it should also provide technologies for service discovery, monitoring and resilience (RQ7).

In order to reduce administrative efforts necessary to create and run arbitrary number of lab instances, the system should integrate with pre-existing authentication infrastructure (e.g., Lightweight Directory Access Protocol (LDAP)) (RQ8).

IV. System Architecture

The eduDScloud in its current implementation is based on VMware vCloud Director (vCD) [8] and accompanying products like ESXi (Hypervisor) and vSphere, due to pre-existing infrastructure and experience using this technology stack. As this introduces certain platform-specific limitations and requirements, the architectural concept of the eduDScloud system (see Figure 1) has been designed such as to prevent a vendor lock-in. This is achieved by avoiding dependencies on platform-specific features where possible, keeping the concept and major parts of lab setups – especially the virtual machines themselves – portable between different vendors.

A lab in vCD is reflected in the form of a vApp, which consists of one or more VMs (RQ1) and their networking – including internal networks as well as connectivity to external networks. Each lab therefore has its own internal network connecting its VMs to each other (RQ3) without any of them being directly accessible from outside the lab. The only exception to this is a pfSense-based [9] gateway VM present in all eduDScloud labs, which acts as a gateway and OpenVPN server, allowing students to join the internal network and providing access to the internet (RQ4).

Connectivity between otherwise independent vApps can be provided by addition of a *CommonServices* vApp to a lecture, which will create site-to-site VPN connections to all other labs in the lecture. While *CommonServices* can itself provide additional services, its pfSense instance also allows connected labs to offer services using network address translation (RQ5).

Both vCD and pfSense allow the use of authentication providers (RQ8) – like the LDAP infrastructure present at the University of Applied Sciences and Arts Hannover– with the eduDScloud using the permission system within vCD to manage authorization as the directory is provided as read-only resource. Permissions for individual vApps are then synced to the respective pfSense instances using a Java client which accesses the vCD API. As an alternative approach, authorization could be handled completely via LDAP – even if the directory used for authentication is read-only – by employing an intermediary identity and access management solution like e.g. Keycloak [10], which is controlled by the eduDScloud administrators.

All vApps are instantiated from templates stored in a catalogue, which can be shared between lectures as necessary. Each template represents a full snapshot of all VMs that are part of a lab, making it easy to deploy additional instances as well as reset existing ones to their original state in case of a fatal misconfiguration (RQ6). As an alternative to this potentially destructive operation, which would result in a loss of all work which has not been backed up beforehand, it is also possible to create snapshots of deployed lab instances before performing risky operations.

V. Microservices Lab

The lab created for teaching microservices is comprised of seven VMs in total, not counting the obligatory gateway VM. While the *Services-ESB* VM is an artifact of the same lab also being used in general SOA exercises, the other six VMs are either dedicated for use with a microservice architecture based on the Netflix Open Source Software stack (Netflix OSS) [11] or at least intended for dual-use to save resources.

A. Netflix OSS Stack

With regards to open source microservice stacks, Netflix OSS is mentioned by [7] for its easy accessibility on the implementation side through Spring Cloud Netflix and providing many features catering specifically to the needs of microservice architectures. For the sake of reduced complexity

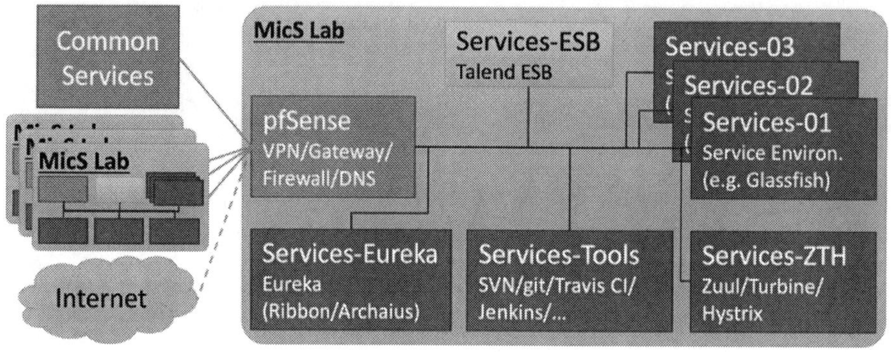

Figure 2. Diagram of the virtual microservices (MicS) lab showing all VMs and their connectivity with services and networks outside of the lab.

in an educational context, the components can be reduced to a set of four core technologies, crucial for teaching the basic characteristics of microservices (RQ7):

- *Eureka* — Provides a registry which can be used by services to locate other available services; checks availability via heartbeat.
- *Zuul* — The gateway to the entire service architecture; transparently routes requests to available service instances discovered through Eureka.
- *Turbine* — A stream aggregator used to collect metrics from all currently running service instances and make them available to Hystrix.
- *Hystrix* — Increases the architecture's resilience by offering circuit breaking capabilities [6] [12] to trigger fail-fast behaviour for services monitored via Turbine; helps prevent errors in monitored services from cascading across the entire system.

Additional components like Archaius (remote configuration) and Ribbon (load balancer) could be included for certain specific exercise tasks, but would exceed the scope of an introductory lab. Especially Ribbon also provides only very limited advantages in a lab environment, as Zuul already provides basic, round-robin load balancing.

B. VM Configuration

As can be seen in Figure 2, three of the seven VMs in the microservices lab setup are general purpose VMs (*Services-01* through *Services-03*). These VMs contain a basic installation of a Linux system along with a preconfigured application server (Glassfish) and can be increased or decreased in number as required by exercises and projects. While the application server is intended for use in exercises targeting conventional, SOAs based on the use of an enterprise service bus (ESB), these machines can also be used as fully reconfigurable and customisable hosts for individual microservices.

For this purpose, all systems offer a privileged (sudoer; root level access) and an unprivileged user account each, to both of which the students have full access (RQ2). This allows them to not only deploy services to the application server, but also install completely independent technology stacks on each host, e.g., running a Java service using PostgreSQL on one and a .NET Core service backed by a MongoDB on another. While the privileged account is needed for the necessary changes to the system, unprivileged user accounts are to be used to actually run the individual tools and services, teaching students some of the basic best practices in server administration.

One of the fully pre-configured VMs (*Services-ZTH*) in the setup is used to run a Zuul as well as a combined Turbine and Hystrix instance, whose configuration in a simplified lab environment can be considered trivial. The only changes necessary is the addition of new services to the list of monitored ones as students deploy them to their lab.

An additional, stand-alone VM (*Services-Eureka*) acts as the service registry, running a pre-configured Eureka instance, which is already hooked up with Zuul. In addition, this machine also offers basic preparations for deploying Archaius and Ribbon, should specific projects or exercises require them.

To facilitate source code versioning as well as automated build and deployment processes, the *Services-Tools* VM – in its most basic configuration – acts as a Subversion and git host. Depending on the deployment toolchain [13] chosen for the lab, it can quickly be set up to run a choice of build and test automation tools like Jenkins or Travis CI. When the lab is run with a focus on conventional SOA meanwhile, this host also acts as a database server, allowing *Services-ZTH* and *Services-Eureka* to be shut down in order to save resources.

The last VM in the lab's line-up is *Services-ESB*, which – in its current configuration – runs an instance of the Talend ESB, capable of deploying OSGi containers via Apache Karaf. This combination of ESB-based SOA and technologies focused on microservices within a single lab allows lecturers to not only teach these concepts independently from each other, but also in tandem, e.g., in the form of integration challenges.

C. First Experiences with the Lab

The current setup running at the University of Applied Sciences and Arts Hannover includes total of 28 cores (48 threads), having access to 512 GB of RAM and 40 TB of storage for the actual cloud itself. The management server, which is running infrastructure services like vCloud, vSphere, vShield (networking), pfSense (DNS and DHCP) and a backup solution called Veeam [14], is equipped with 4 cores (8 threads), 32 GB of RAM and 4 TB HDD storage. For backups, additional space is supplied by a QNAP storage array providing an additional 8 TB of disk space, to which snapshots of the management VMs and lab templates are written.

Due to the number of VMs contained within a single instance of the virtual microservices lab, the number of cores in the initial hardware setup has turned out to quickly become an issue. With between three to four students per group and each VM (except for the pfSense instance) using two virtual cores (vCores) each, a lecture with 25 students needs about one hundred vCores in total. This makes it impractical to run multiple lectures in parallel on the current hardware, which can be partially alleviated by temporarily suspending labs of other lectures for the duration of certain exercise sessions.

Some issues that occurred during the exercises themselves were, that OpenVPN – used to connect with the virtual lab environments internal network – requires administrative permissions on the client system. Since providing students with root level access to shared pool systems is infeasible, a custom script had to be implemented in order to allow unprivileged users to run OpenVPN using custom configurations and temporarily modify the clients' DNS configuration.

VI. CONCLUSION

The eduDScloud provides a solid, scalable private cloud solution for hosting virtual labs used in teaching microservices and other topics from the field of computer sciences. It allows students to gain hands-on experience by providing them with root access to virtual machines and networks within a sandboxed environment. At the same time, it grants lecturers and tutors the ability to devise more complex exercise tasks with a minimum of administrative work as new labs can easily be instantiated from pre-built templates.

A specialised lab setup has been presented as an example for a virtual lab running on the eduDScloud, used to teach concepts of SOA in general and microservices in specific. This lab provides students with a preconfigured stack for ESB-based service development as well as running the Netflix OSS stack to showcase microservice-specific technologies and patterns. The presence of both stacks in a single lab, along with the interconnectivity of deployed lab instances also opens up opportunities for integration exercises between student groups, which represent a common real-world use case for service-oriented architectures.

VII. FUTURE WORK

While the eduDScloud is already capable of scaling out across multiple servers, its current implementation limits it to private cloud capabilities. This can become especially challenging when, e.g., due to scheduling issues, a high number of lab instances has to run in parallel, potentially exceeding the computing resources of the available hardware. To alleviate these issues, upcoming projects include migrating the eduDScloud towards a hybrid cloud concept, allowing it to scale out using public cloud resources on demand, while maintaining privacy protection for sensitive applications.

Part of this migration is the evaluation of open-source virtualisation platforms and frameworks such as Proxmox [15] and especially OpenStack [16], as the latter would allow seamless integration with various public cloud providers. Switching to one of these solutions would also allow for the entire stack of the eduDScloud to be running solely on open-source software, as VMware components are currently the only proprietary, closed-source part of the system.

In addition to this, further research topics include the development of new lab concepts for other fields of computer science, increasing the platform's resilience and improving resource scheduling. The latter is currently handled manually and is planned to be automated by synchronising it with a live schedule for labs and lectures, and integrating it with a reservation platform to handle projects and other activities.

ACKNOWLEDGEMENT

The authors would like to thank the students which were part of the combined bachelor and master project during the winter and summer semester 2016/2017 for their contribution to the implementation of the eduDScloud.

REFERENCES

[1] J. Fenn. 2010 Emerging Technologies Hype Cycle is Here - Mastering The Hype Cycle. [retrieved: 2018-01-05]. [Online]. Available: https://blogs.gartner.com/hypecyclebook/2010/09/07/2010-emerging-technologies-hype-cycle-is-here/ (2010)

[2] Google. Higher Ed G Suite — Google for Education. [retrieved: 2018-01-05]. [Online]. Available: https://edu.google.com/higher-ed-solutions/g-suite/

[3] S. S. Foley, D. Koepke, J. Ragatz, C. Brehm, J. Regina, and J. Hursey, "Onramp: A web-portal for teaching parallel and distributed computing," Journal of Parallel and Distributed Computing, vol. 105, 2017, pp. 138–149.

[4] K. Chine, "Learning math and statistics on the cloud, towards an ec2-based google docs-like portal for teaching / learning collaboratively with r and scilab," in 2010 10th IEEE International Conference on Advanced Learning Technologies. IEEE, 2010, pp. 752–753.

[5] F. Doelitzscher, A. Sulistio, C. Reich, H. Kuijs, and D. Wolf, "Private cloud for collaboration and e-learning services: From iaas to saas," Computing, vol. 91, no. 1, 2011, pp. 23–42.

[6] S. Newman, Building Microservices, 1st ed. Sebastopol: O'Reilly & Associates, 2015.

[7] E. Wolff, Microservices: Grundlagen flexibler Softwarearchitekturen, 1st ed. Heidelberg: dpunkt.verlag, 2016.

[8] VMware. Deliver Virtual Data Centers — vCloud Director — VMware. [retrieved: 2018-01-05]. [Online]. Available: https://www.vmware.com/products/vcloud-director.html

[9] Rubicon Communications. pfSense - World's Most Trusted Open Source Firewall. [retrieved: 2018-01-05]. [Online]. Available: https://www.pfsense.org

[10] I. Red Hat. Keycloak. [retrieved: 2018-01-05]. [Online]. Available: http://www.keycloak.org

[11] Netflix. Netflix Open Source. [retrieved: 2018-01-05]. [Online]. Available: https://netflix.github.io

[12] S. J. Fowler, Production-ready microservices: Building standardized systems across an engineering organization, first edition ed. Beijing and Boston and Farnham and Sebastopol and Tokyo: O'Reilly, 2016.

[13] T. Hunter II, Advanced Microservices: A Hands-on Approach to Microservice Infrastructure and Tooling, 1st ed. New York: APRESS, 2017.

[14] Veeam Software. Veeam Availability for the Always-On Enterprise. [retrieved: 2018-01-05]. [Online]. Available: https://www.veeam.com

[15] Proxmox Server Solutions GmbH. Proxmox - powerful open-source server solutions. [retrieved: 2018-01-05]. [Online]. Available: https://www.proxmox.com/en/

[16] OpenStack Foundation. Openstack Open Source Cloud Computing Software. [retrieved: 2018-01-05]. [Online]. Available: https://www.openstack.org

A Service Based Architecture for Situation-Aware Adaptive Event Stream Processing

Marc Schaaf

University of Applied Sciences Northwestern Switzerland,
Riggenbachstr. 16, 4600 Olten, Switzerland
Email: marc.schaaf@fhnw.ch

***Abstract*—This paper presents the central aspects of a service based architecture for a distributed event stream processing system with an emphasis on its components, as well as related scalability and flexibility considerations. The processing system architecture is designed based on a well-defined situation-aware adaptive event stream processing model and a matching scenario definition language, which allow the definition of such processing scenarios in a processing system independent way.**

Keywords–Event Stream Processing; Microservices; Service-oriented Architecture; Publish-Subscribe

I. Introduction

Event Stream Processing (ESP) applications play an important role in modern information systems due to their capability to rapidly analyze huge amounts of information and to quickly react based on the results. They follow the approach to produce notifications based on state changes (e.g., stock value changes) represented by events, which actively trigger further processing tasks. They contrast to the typical store and process approaches where data is gathered and processed later in a batch processing fashion, which typically involves a higher latency. Event Stream Processing applications can achieve scalability even for huge amounts of streaming event data by partitioning incoming data streams and assigning them to multiple machines for parallel processing. Due to those properties, Event Stream Processing based analytical systems are likely to have a further increasing relevance in future IT systems. Also, it is likely that future ESP applications will have to handle even larger amounts of data while taking on increasingly complex processing tasks to allow for near real-time analytics to take place.

An example for such a scenario is the detection and tracing of solar energy production drops caused by clouds shading solar panels as they pass by [1]. The scenario requires a processing system to handle large amounts of streaming data to (1) detect a possible cloud (a possible situation), to (2) verify the possible situation and (3) to track the changes of the situation as the cloud moves or changes its size or shape. For the initial detection of a potential situation, a processing system needs to analyze the energy production of all monitored solar panel installations. However, for the second part, the verification of a potential cloud, only a situation specific subset of the monitoring data is needed. In the same way, the later tracking of the situation only requires a situation specific subset, which may change over time.

In order to handle such large numbers of events, a processing system needs to be capable of distributing the processing across several machines. A common mechanism for the distribution is to partition the overall data stream [2]. When a processing system partitions the incoming data streams in order to achieve scalability, such a partitioning will be suitable for the first part of the processing, the detection of a potential situation as the partitioning is *situation independent*. For the later processing part where a *situation specific* subset of the incoming data streams is required, a general stream partitioning scheme based on for example the processing system load, is not suitable as it does not incorporate the needs of currently analyzed situations. Here, a dynamic adaptation mechanism is needed that takes the investigated situations state into account.

This paper presents the central aspects of a microservice based architecture for a distributed event stream processing system that implements the afore mentioned processing model. The discussions put a specific emphasis on the architectures components, as well as related scalability and flexibility due to the realization as microservices based on the OSGi framework.

The remainder of this paper is structured as follows: The next section discusses the related work, followed by a presentation of the processing model in Section II to lay the foundation for Section III which discusses the goals of the here presented processing system architecture. Section IV then presents the architecture and its components. Before concluding the paper in Section VI, Section V discusses several development related aspects towards the presented architecture.

II. Related Work

Various systems for distributing a processing system in order to provide the needed scalability exist like Aurora* and Borealis [3][4]. Aurora* for example starts with a very crude data stream partitioning in the beginning and tries to optimize its processing system over time based on the gathered resource usage statistics [5]. Furthermore, various approaches have been proposed which employ adaptive optimizations to handle load fluctuations by utilizing the dynamic resource availability of cloud computing offerings like [6][7][8] in order to scale on demand. Other approaches introduce new operators which allow for an adaptive partitioning or query plan execution. For example the Flux operator [9] allows for a dynamic partitioning of state-full operators during run-time in order to flexibly scale a stream processing system to handle varying processing loads. An even more flexible version is the Eddy operator which was proposed by Avnur et al. [10]. The Eddy operator allows for a continuous reordering of the operators in a query plan during run-time. The approach considers the query plan as a task where tuples need to be routed through the operators. Within this model, the Eddy operator allows a per-tuple routing decision thus allowing for a fine-grained control of the actual query graph during run-time. An application of the Eddy operator to continuous queries exists with the Continuous Adaptive Continuous Queries over Streams (CACQ) [11].

In general, the here discussed systems are capable of setting up distributed stream processing based on given queries and to optimize the system to provide the required processing capacity and response times. However, the systems have no mechanisms to adapt deployed stream queries based on detected situations and situation changes as they have no knowledge of the overall analytical task that deployed a given stream query.

III. Processing Model and Language

We approach the outlined problem by defining a *situation-aware adaptive stream processing model* together with a matching *scenario definition language* to allow the definition of such processing scenarios for a scenario independent processing system [12][13][14]. The requirements for the definition of the model and language are the result of an analysis of several scenarios from two application domains, telecommunications network and Smart Grid monitoring.

The designed model defines situation aware adaptive processing in three main phases (Figure 1):

- Phase 1: In the *Possible Situation Indication* phase, possible situations are detected in a large set of streaming data, were the focus lies on the rapid processing of large amounts of data, explicitly accepting the generation of false positives and duplicate notifications over precise calculations.
- Phase 2: The *Focused Situation Processing Initialization* phase determines whether an indicated possible situation needs to be investigated or if it can be ignored, for example because the situation was already under investigation. If a potential situation needs to be investigated, a new situation specific focused processing is started.
- Phase 3: In the *Focused Situation Processing* phase, possible situations are first verified and then an in-depth investigation of the situation including the adaptation of the processing setup based on interim results is possible.

Based on our processing model we defined the Scenario Processing Template Language (SPTL), which allows the specification of processing templates based on the concepts of the processing model in an implementation independent way.

The SPTL allows the specification of the needed processing steps for each phase of the processing model. To allow the specification, it embeds several other languages:

- SPARQL [15] is used as the query language to retrieve background knowledge on the monitored system.
- MVEL [16] is used as an expression and scripting language.
- DROOLS [17] is used to specify the actual stream processing rules.

Furthermore, the SPTL allows the specification of variables which can be embedded and into the sub-languages in order to share processing results. Moreover, simple procedural statements can be made in SPTL.

In order to evaluate the processing model and language, a processing system prototype was developed. The following sections discuss the architecture of this processing system.

IV. Architecture Goals and Resulting Architecture Decisions

The two main aspects considered for the design of the here presented architecture are the scalability and the flexibility of the architecture. With regard to the scalability, the following aspects were considered:

- Handling of a large set of input streams that need to be monitored for potential situations.
- Detection and processing of many parallel situations.

The other main aspect considered is the flexibility with regard to the replacement and adaptation of components during development and while testing:

- *Adaptability of components:* The replacement of components in order to test and evaluate new concepts (interfaces came from shared library ensuring that interface changes can be made at one central place)
- *Local and distributed operation*: The integration with local test environment on developer system, as well as integration with a distributed test environment and the later deployment in a productive environment

While the mentioned aspects regarding the scalability of the processing system were also considered for the design of the processing model, the second aspect was only considered for the design of the processing system architecture. Thus, this paper focuses the discussions on the second aspect, the flexibility of the architecture.

V. Processing System Architecture

The overall processing system was subdivided into several components (Figure 2), each with distinct functionality. For the communication between the components interfaces were defined, which depending on the communication need are implemented as synchronous service based interactions or asynchronous message based interactions.

The following discussion will first outline the functionality of the supporting components. Then the four main components implementing the processing model are presented.

A. Background Knowledge Base (KB)

The processing model defines, that background knowledge on the monitored system can be retrieved for the set-up of the possible indication stream processing, as well as the later focused situation processing. The KB component provides access to this background knowledge. As the processing model only allows read only queries against the KB, the component can easily be scaled out onto multiple machines.

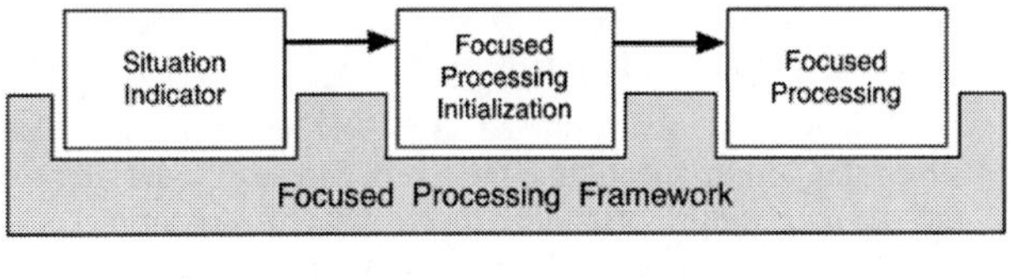

Figure 1. Three phases of the Processing Model

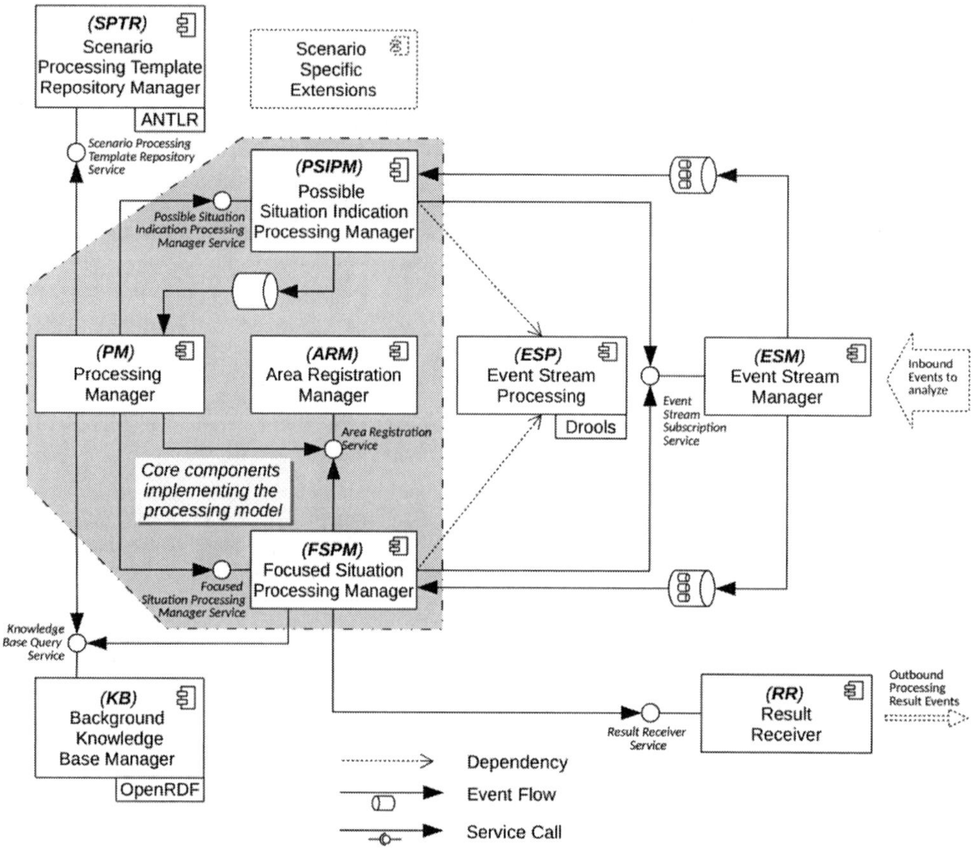

Figure 2. Architecture: Module View [14]

B. Scenario Processing Template Repository Manager (SPTR)

The SPTR is responsible for reading scenario processing templates specified in the SPTL, parsing them and performing an initial validation of the provided templates. The loaded templates can then be retrieved by the provided Scenario Processing Template Repository Service.

1) Event Stream Manager (ESM): The ESM allows other components to request data streams where the data streams can be live data streams or historic data delivered as a steam. When a component requests a certain data stream, the ESM responds with a handle to a messaging channel where the requesting component then subscribes to in order to receive the requested data stream.

2) Result Receiver (RR): The RR receives final or interim processing results in order to deliver them to a foreign system. As such different implementations of this component exist for a simple testing environment, where results are written to file or a live system where the results are for example forwarded to a decision support system.

Aside from the discussed components, there are further supporting components like the Event Stream Processing module or a module providing user defined scenario specific extensions. These components are used as shared libraries, providing an implementation of common functionality for the active components.

Based on these supporting components, the afore mentioned processing model is implemented. In order to allow for a distributed operation, the processing model itself is distributed across the following four components, each with a distinct functionality defined by the processing model:

C. Possible Situation Indication Processing Manager (PSIPM)

The PSIPM implements the functionality to instantiate a static stream processing network based on a provided stream processing topology specification. As such it interacts with the Event Stream Manager (ESM) where it subscribes to the required event streams. As the processing model does not allow any access to background knowledge during the indication stream processing, the PSIPM does not need access to the KB.

D. Focused Situation Processing Manager (FSPM)

The FSPM implements the actual situation specific analysis by providing the means to instantiate multiple situation focused processing tasks upon request. Each processing task investigates a single situation by implementing an iterative processing mechanism where each of these iterations follows a fixed process involving a preparation, a stream processing and a reasoning phase in order to conclude on interim processing results and to define the adaptation of the processing instance for the next iteration. The actual processing within each step is specified by the user in the corresponding scenario processing template.

As multiple parallel processing tasks are executed in parallel, a synchronization between these instances is realized based on the Area Registration mechanism discussed in Section V-F.

The two afore discussed components, PSIPM and FSPM, both implement the actual stream processing tasks within this processing model. As they are decoupled from the rest of the processing system except from a very limited set of well-defined services, the stream processing can be implemented based on various technologies, based on the actual requirements from a given application domain. While the current implementation of these components utilizes JBoss Drools Fusion [17], an alternative implementation could for example utilize an Apache Spark [18] based cluster to realize the stream processing and thereby greatly enhance the scalability of the processing system.

E. Processing Manager (PM)

The PM acts as a stateful overseer component for the three phases of the processing model. It thus coordinates the initial set-up of the processing system for a given scenario. Further, for Phase 2 it implements the decision process regarding the instantiation of new situation specific processing tasks. The actual stream processing needed for Phase 1 and 3 are delegated to separate components.

For the initial set-up of processing tasks, the PM retrieves the list of available scenario processing templates from the SPTR component, executes the contained definitions for the Phase 1 processing (possible situation indication processing) to generate the stream processing topology definition for the given scenario. Once the topology was generated, the PM hands the topology definition to the PSIPM which in turn instantiates the topology and starts with the stream processing. When handing over the topology description, the PM also provides the PSIPM with a handle for a messaging channel where the PM listens for generated possible situation indication events published by the PSIPM upon the detection of a new possible situation.

When the PM receives a new possible situation indication event, it needs to decide if the event regards a new possible situation or an already investigated situation. The decision is implemented by the PM based on a set of user defined rules from the corresponding scenario processing template. Furthermore, the system needs to keep track of already active situation processing tasks and the situations under investigation. This tracking is implemented through an area registration mechanism which also acts as the main synchronization point for the processing system (discussed in the next section). If the PM decides that a new possible situation was detected, it requests the instantiation of the new Focused Situation Processing instance from the FSPM. If the event was deemed related to an existing situation, the PM delegates the event to the corresponding, already running, Focused Situation Processing Instance.

F. Area Registration Manager (ARM)

The processing model defines the Area Registration mechanism as the central synchronization mechanism between the processing Phase 2 and 3. An Area Registration is defined as a tuple consisting of two sets of nodes, the *Locked Area* LA and the *Focus Area* FA combined with the time frame tf of the registrations validity and a reference to the owner of the registration, a Focused Situation Processing Instance fpi:

$$ar := (LA, FL, tf, fpi)$$

The processing model then requires that at all nodes of any Locked Area LA may only be owned by a single Area Registration within the registration's validity time frame tf. Based on this mechanism, the processing model implements the synchronization between multiple parallel processing tasks. This synchronization is implemented by the ARM which keeps track of all active registration and is the single component with the authority to grant new area registrations. As such, the ARM is a crucial component for the whole processing system making its efficient implementation essential for the scalability of the overall processing system. For the current prototype, a simple Java based implementation of the ARM exists. However, for larger systems, a more optimized version which also considers for example the partitioning of the registrations in order to provide a distributed implementation should be considered. As all access to this component is also well-defined through a limited number of service based interactions, such a replacement would have no impact on the other components.

VI. Development Considerations

We based the processing system on the OSGi module framework where typically each component from the architecture became an OSGi bundle. Aside from the separation of the components as OSGi bundles, the OSGi framework also allowed for service based interactions between these bundles. This allowed the development of the processing system as an at first non distributed version running in a single Java Virtual Machine while for later distributed deployments, the OSGi Remote Services could be used. As distributed message based communication was not supported by OSGi at the time the system was implemented, we utilized the integration mechanism presented in [19].

Moreover, OSGi allowed for the replacement of components during runtime, which eased the development of the processing system and resulted in a more robust system with regard to the handling of service or component availabilities as components and services where often removed and replaced during runtime even while developing the system on a local machine.

Even though this approach allowed the development of a component based system, one of the larger challenges during the early versions of the processing system was the lack of traceability between components. This in particular with regard to the asynchronous message based interactions. We mitigated this problem by enforcing data types for the messaging integration which allowed for a limited traceability based on the data types.

In order to ensure that some basic functionality of the system was given even after larger changes, automatic integration tests where implemented as part of the build process for a small set of test scenarios. These tests turned out to be very fragile during the early development as still concepts of the model and language changed frequently. However, they also ensured that even after a change in the processing model, the processing system was still capable to provide the processing capabilities needed for some basic scenarios, thus allowing for more confidence in the processing system even as larger changes occurred which regarded multiple components.

VII. Conclusions

The paper presents a highly modular service based architecture for realizing a processing system for situation-aware adaptive event stream processing. The architecture distributes the main parts of the situation aware processing model into four components, each with distinct functionalities. Further all supporting functionality is provided by separate components. All interactions between the components are defined either as service based or message based interactions which allows the components to be replaced independently.

By using the OSGi framework for the development of the processing system prototype we were able to develop this highly modularized, service based system locally in a single Java Runtime while retaining the possibility to distribute the prototype later based on the OSGi Remote Services.

Due to the design of the architecture together with the usage of the OSGi framework for the implementation, we could achieve the afore mentioned goals, for the development and testing of the system to allow for an easy adaptability of components in order to develop details of processing model and allow for integration into different environments, as well as allowing for a local and distributed mode to ease the development.

Acknowledgements

Parts of the here presented work was done as part of the Eurostars Project E!7377.

References

[1] G. Wilke et al., "Intelligent dynamic load management based on solar panel monitoring," in Proceedings of the 3rd Conference on Smart Grids and Green IT Systems, 2014, pp. 76–81.

[2] M. Hirzel, R. Soulé, S. Schneider, B. Gedik, and R. Grimm, "A Catalog of Stream Processing Optimizations," ACM Comput. Surv., vol. 46, no. 4, mar 2014, pp. 46–1. [Online]. Available: {http://doi.acm.org/10.1145/2528412}

[3] D. J. Abadi et al., "The Design of the Borealis Stream Processing Engine," in In CIDR, 2005, pp. 277–289.

[4] Y. Xing, S. Zdonik, and J.-H. Hwang, "Dynamic Load Distribution in the Borealis Stream Processor," in Proceedings of the 21st International Conference on Data Engineering, ser. ICDE '05. Washington, DC, USA: IEEE Computer Society, 2005, pp. 791–802.

[5] M. Cherniack et al., "Scalable distributed stream processing," in In CIDR, vol. 3, 2003, pp. 257–268.

[6] V. Gulisano, R. Jimenez-Peris, M. Patino-Martinez, and P. Valduriez, "StreamCloud: A Large Scale Data Streaming System," in Distributed Computing Systems (ICDCS), 2010 IEEE 30th International Conference on, june 2010, pp. 126–137.

[7] S. Schneider, H. Andrade, B. Gedik, A. Biem, and K.-L. Wu, "Elastic scaling of data parallel operators in stream processing," in Parallel Distributed Processing, 2009. IPDPS 2009. IEEE International Symposium on, may 2009, pp. 1–12.

[8] W. Kleiminger, E. Kalyvianaki, and P. Pietzuch, "Balancing load in stream processing with the cloud," in Proceedings of the 2011 IEEE 27th International Conference on Data Engineering Workshops, ser. ICDEW '11. Washington, DC, USA: IEEE Computer Society, 2011, pp. 16–21. [Online]. Available: {http://dx.doi.org/10.1109/ICDEW.2011.5767653}

[9] M. A. Shah, J. M. Hellerstein, S. Chandrasekaran, and M. J. Franklin, "Flux: an adaptive partitioning operator for continuous query systems," in Data Engineering, 2003. Proceedings. 19th International Conference on, March 2003, pp. 25–36.

[10] R. Avnur and J. M. Hellerstein, "Eddies: Continuously Adaptive Query Processing," in Proceedings of the 2000 ACM SIGMOD International Conference on Management of Data, ser. SIGMOD '00. New York, NY, USA: ACM, 2000, pp. 261–272. [Online]. Available: {http://doi.acm.org/10.1145/342009.335420}

[11] S. Madden, M. Shah, J. M. Hellerstein, and V. Raman, "Continuously Adaptive Continuous Queries over Streams," in Proceedings of the 2002 ACM SIGMOD International Conference on Management of Data, ser. SIGMOD '02. New York, NY, USA: ACM, 2002, pp. 49–60. [Online]. Available: {http://doi.acm.org/10.1145/564691.564698}

[12] M. Schaaf, "Event processing with dynamically changing focus: Doctoral consortium paper," in RCIS, ser. IEEE 7th International Conference on Research Challenges in Information Science, RCIS 2013, Paris, France, May 29-31, 2013, R. Wieringa, S. Nurcan, C. Rolland, and J.-L. Cavarero, Eds. IEEE, 2013, pp. 1–6.

[13] M. Schaaf et al., "Towards a timely root cause analysis for complex situations in large scale telecommunications networks," Procedia Computer Science, vol. 60, 2015, pp. 160–169, knowledge-Based and Intelligent Information & Engineering Systems 19th Annual Conference, KES-2015, Singapore, September 2015 Proceedings.

[14] M. Schaaf, "Situation aware adaptive event stream processing. a processing model and scenario definition language," Ph.D. dissertation, Technical University Clausthal, 2017, verlag Dr. Hut, ISBN: 978-3-8439-3376-6.

[15] T. W. S. W. Group, "SPARQL 1.1 Overview," Tech. Rep., march 2013, retrieved: 13.01.18. [Online]. Available: https://www.w3.org/TR/2013/REC-sparql11-overview-20130321/

[16] "MVEL Language Guide for 2.0," Online: http://mvel.documentnode.com/, retrieved: 13.01.18.

[17] "Drools Business Rules Management System," Online: http://www.drools.org/, retrieved: 13.01.18.

[18] "Apache Spark Streaming," Online: https://spark.apache.org/streaming/, retrieved: 13.01.18.

[19] M. Schaaf et al., "Integrating asynchronous communication into the osgi service platform," in WEBIST'11, 2011, pp. 165–168.

Service Quality Modeling

Janusz H. Klink
Telecommunications and Teleinformatics Department
Wroclaw University of Science and Technology
Wroclaw, Poland
e-mail: janusz.klink@pwr.edu.pl

Abstract— **The paper presents the selected issues of service quality modeling. The author presents a classification of the main phenomena connected with quality from both the provider's and the user's point of view. It is underlined that service quality will be one of the main issues of next generation networks, like 5G, where the user's perspective will be of a great importance. The main contribution of the paper is the presentation of the method of building the Quality of Experience (QoE) models, based on two popular services, i.e., messaging and web browsing. The author emphasizes that some existing QoE models based on average values do not reflect users' expectations and there is a need for building new, more sophisticated models, which take into account more parameters and also their transient behaviors.**

Keywords-Service quality; QoS; QoE; quality model.

I. INTRODUCTION

The rapid development of current Information and Communication Technologies (ICT) applies not only to the improving of the telecommunication networks infrastructure, but also to the service provision process.

For the last several years, service quality has become more and more important.

The term 'quality', as defined in an International Standards Organization (ISO) document [1], means 'the totality of characteristics of an entity that bear on its ability to satisfy stated and implied needs'. Based on this, the International Telecommunication Union (ITU) formulated the definition of Quality of Service (QoS), as 'the collective effect of service performances that determine the degree of satisfaction of a user of the service' [2].

For many years, a major effort was concentrated on ensuring a high level of network performance parameters. Thus, the operator was perceived as the main subject responsible for the quality of services provided to the users. Such an approach was often justified, because the network operator (NO) played the role of the service provider (SP), and was therefore the main actor in the service delivery chain.

Nowadays, in most cases, these two roles are separated. Moreover, users connect to the services via networks, which are managed by many different NOs.

Figure 1 presents different viewpoints on service quality, taking into account the relationships between the end-user (customer) and the service provider; it is based on a QoS framework presented by ITU-T in G.1000 Recommendation [3]. A very similar approach can be found in [4].

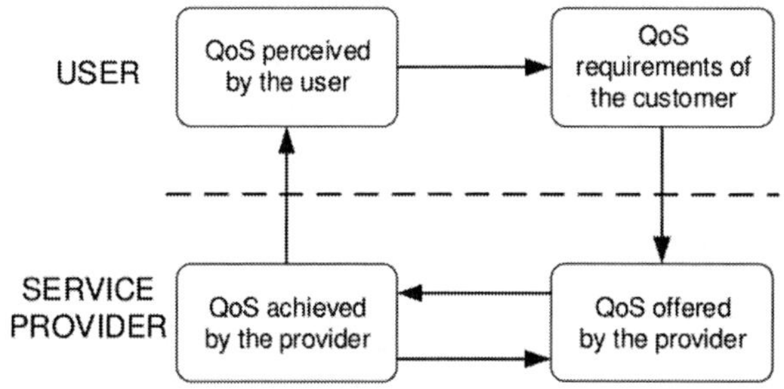

Figure 1. Different viewpoints of QoS [3].

The upper part of the Figure 1 presents the user's point of view on the QoS, while the bottom part shows the problem from the provider's perspective. Every user has his own requirements concerning the specific service. These requirements are manifested to the provider and may be expressed in non-technical language. The customers are not usually familiar with the technical specifications of the service and they are not concerned with how the services are provided. Instead of the technical aspects of the design of the network, users are concerned with the final result, i.e., end-to-end (e2e) service quality. Service quality, as seen by the user, focuses on user-perceived effects and does not take any assumptions about the internal design of the network or performance indicators. The user's needs are described in network-independent terms using a common language, which is understandable by both the user and the service provider. The QoS offered by the SP is a statement of the level of quality that is expected to be offered to the customer [3]. It is expressed by the values assigned to QoS parameters. Each service should be described by its own set of parameters. The principal use of such a form of QoS is for network and Service Level Agreements (SLAs) planning. It is often defined in a statistical manner where the average, minimum and maximum values of the parameters play an important role.

It is also very important for the service provider to achieve the same level of quality that was previously offered. Moreover, the most important is the QoS perceived by the users. The quality here is often expressed in terms of degrees of satisfaction, which are usually not technical terms. It is assessed by customer surveys and from their own comments on levels of service. Perceived QoS can be used by the service provider to determine the customer satisfaction of service quality. A high level of the quality perceived by the user influences his expectations for the future. It usually causes an increase in user demands addressed to the SP.

The rest of this paper is organized as follows. In Section 2, the author presents a more detailed classification of the service quality approaches and also the main objective and subjective factors which influence the quality experienced by users. Section 3, presents the main factors that really concern users in the scope of QoE. It shows which factors are the most important for the average user and they are then taken into account during the quality assessment. It gives information about the important parameters that should be primarily measured and controlled. Section 4, discusses the problem of building the QoE models and presents some results. At the end, in Section 5, the author summarizes the whole work and presents some challenging problems that should be solved in order to improve the service QoE modeling process.

II. Quality

In [5], a general model of the QoS was presented. The author distinguishes three dimensions of quality. The first one is called '*Intrinsic QoS*', which relates to its technical characteristics and is determined by the design of the transport network design and the provisioning of network access, terminations and connections. The required quality can be achieved by, among others, the appropriate selection of transport protocols and QoS assurance mechanisms. The intrinsic QoS rating cannot be influenced by user perception. The second dimension of the quality is that of perceived QoS, which reflects the user's (customer's) experience of using a service. It is influenced by his expectations when compared to observed service performance. These expectations are usually affected by the user's experience with a similar telecommunications service, and also other customers' opinions. It can be seen that different users may have their own expectations of the service and the same intrinsic quality may not guarantee the same level of user satisfaction [6].

Figure 2 shows the general QoS model according to ITU/ETSI and IETF approaches [6].

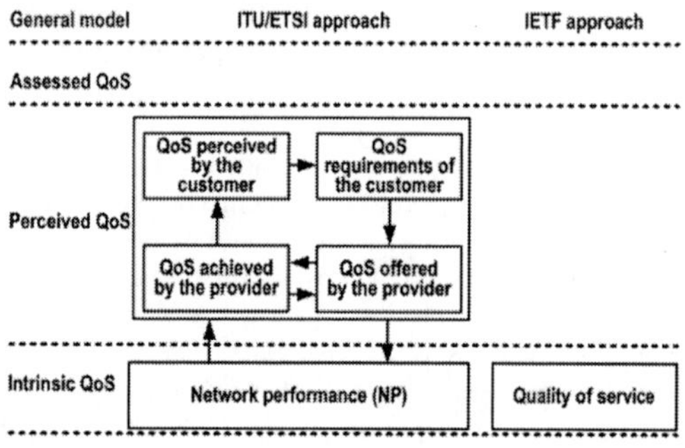

Figure 2. The general quality model - ITU-T/ETSI and IETF approaches.

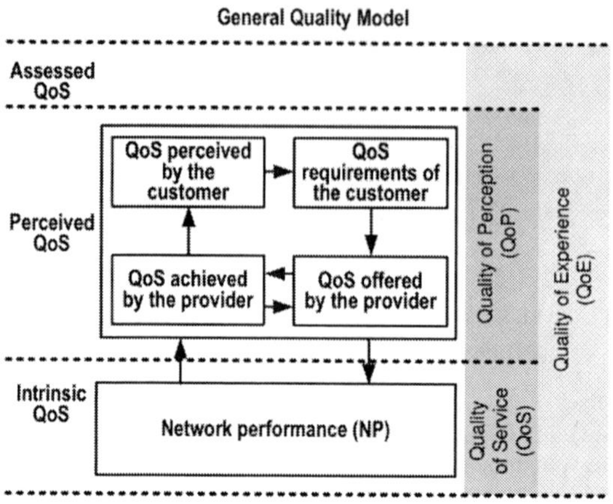

Figure 3. An amendment to the general quality model.

The provider must also take into consideration nontechnical parameters that are meaningful to the users in order to ensure a high level of assessed QoS, which is exposed when a user decides whether to continue using a service [5]. Sometimes 'intrinsic QoS', according to the ETSI approach, is called QoS and instead of 'perceived QoS' the term 'Quality of Perception' (QoP) is used. The 'assessed QoS', in turn, evolves towards the so-called Quality of Experience (QoE) and may be treated as a resultant of all the technical and nontechnical parameters influencing the service quality experienced by the user (Figure 3).

The approach presented in Figure 3, especially with regards to the intrinsic QoS, is not complete because it only shows the influence of transport factors (network performance) on the quality perceived by the end user. These factors are in the scope of the NO's responsibility.

The fact is that other factors also have an impact on QoP. These are service and application factors. The first one is in the scope of the SP's liability, while the second one depends on the user's equipment. Therefore, there is a need to strengthen efforts in all three of these areas, i.e., service provision, network performance and the end-user's application capability, in order to achieve a warm appreciation of the service quality perceived by the users.

As mentioned above (see Figure 3), the final user's decision in terms of using a specific service in the future is QoE. The problem is, that end-users themselves are not really uniform with respect to their QoE requirements, which

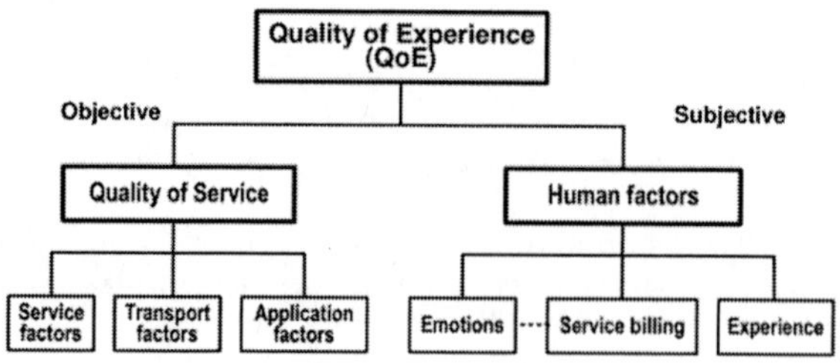

Figure 4. Quality of Experience components.

may be affected by their prior knowledge and expectations, along with the current usage context. All these factors have a strong influence on their QoE needs [7]. Figure 4 presents key subjective (human) factors that, together with objective ones, form the whole picture of QoE.

III. What Matters in Quality Assessment

Service quality will become more and more important, not only for existing services, but also for new emerging technologies and services on the Information and Communications Technology (ICT) market. One of the most awaited solutions is a fifth-generation mobile network (5G), which is expected to be operational by 2020 [8]. It is assumed that it will integrate new applications and services as well as evolved versions of existing ones [9].

5G is a system both for things and for human-centric devices and services. It is envisioned as a system to serve both the user and society. What makes 5G different from previous generations of communication networks is that it will not be designed to offer fixed values of data rates anywhere, anytime and to anyone, but to perform more meaningful, flexible and personalized network management based on the understanding of the end-user's and service's needs [8]. Therefore defining the quality requirements for all users in terms of latency, data rate, coverage, reliability, security, etc. is important, however, more attention should be paid to individual user QoE. Thus, satisfying the users' requirements implies the necessity to move from a system-centric to a more user- (or human-) centric design. In order to do this we first have to understand what users really want.

Future 5G networks will be characterized by high bandwidth with speeds in excess of 10 Gb/s, various mobility levels, and energy and cost-efficient solutions with the augmentation of the wireless world's intelligence, but they should also meet the satisfaction of users. The main challenges for 5G technology are the greatly increased amount of data generated by evolved applications, a massive number of devices to connect to different radio-access technologies, and the need for high quality services [22]. The 5G will be a heterogeneous network architecture consisting of a mixed use of infrastructure elements such as macro-cells, micro-cells, and pico-femto-cells based on interworking different cellular and wireless local area network standards. Emerging monitor and control applications with very low wireless data rates combined with very low energy consumption and with ultra-low latency (<1 ms) are expected to be components of 5G systems.

A new problem with QoE arises from the fact that different users, services and applications have different requirements [10]. Thus, customer personalization and services differentiation mechanisms should be implemented in emerging technologies (e.g., 5G) to ensure high level of QoE.

As was mentioned in the previous section, QoE may be affected by a lot of factors. It is valuable to know which of them really concern users in terms of service quality. In a recent study [11], the most important were the following: reliability (47%), coverage (36%), data speed (9%) or other (5%). It means that users, first of all, care about reliability, i.e., consistency in their perceived experience. Consistency refers to the uninterrupted, seamless and nearly invariable excellent service quality. It spans across different dimensions, like time, space, network infrastructure, operator, service provider and end-user equipment (hardware and application software) [8].

The second important factor describing the quality experienced by users is coverage, i.e., availability of the service. Data speed is located in third place. A relatively low number of respondents mentioning it among meaningful parameters indicates that this factor is far less important than the previous ones. This is information for SPs and NOs on what kind of factors should be recognized as the Key Performance Indicators (KPIs) that influence users' QoE. As a consequence, these indicators should be first and foremost measured.

IV. QoE Models - Case Studies

When it comes to a specific service, it is important to recognize what kind of KPIs really matter to the customers who use the service, and how these KPIs influence the service quality experienced by them. In other words, it is a problem of building proper QoE models for the individual services. Now, we are witnessing a rapid development of so-called OTT services (Over-The-Top-service), in which customers use applications such as iMessage, WhatsApp, Facebook Messenger, SnapChat etc. and generate a high volume of data traffic where information should be delivered as quickly as possible. Moreover, these applications are not treated as uni- but as bidirectional means of communication (e.g., for chatting), where message delivery time plays a crucial role. One of the applications examined by the author was messaging service [12]. The tests were done in a laboratory network, where 40 selected users were sending and receiving messages (1200 in total) between each other. A special tool was used to control the network delay. The users were not informed about the delay set-up, but experienced the effects of these activities, i.e., they perceived the occurrence of service interactivity disturbances. After each session, the users were asked to assess the quality of the service based on their recent perception and to give a grade form 1 (the lowest) to 5 (the highest). Each e2e message delivery time was captured and stored in a database. Figure 5 presents the relation between the message delivery time and the users' grades, representing their QoE, in the MOS scale. The single dashed column represents the average value of the users' grades of all the messages that were delivered in a specific time period. The whiskers represent a 95% level of confidence. Statistical analysis showed a significant (~80%) correlation between message delivery times and the users' evaluation grades. Next, regression analysis was performed and, using ordinary least squares (OLS) estimation, the approximate relation between message delivery time and the users' grades (in the MOS scale) was determined as follows:

$$MOS = -0.1\,T + 4.9 \qquad (1)$$

where T – message delivery time.

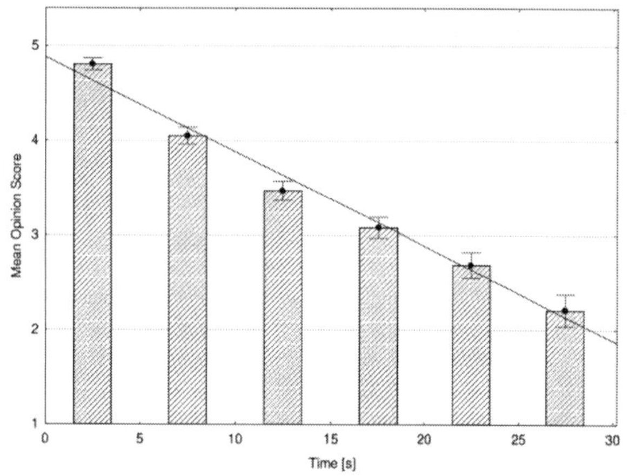

Figure 5. Message delivery time vs. MOS for Messaging service.

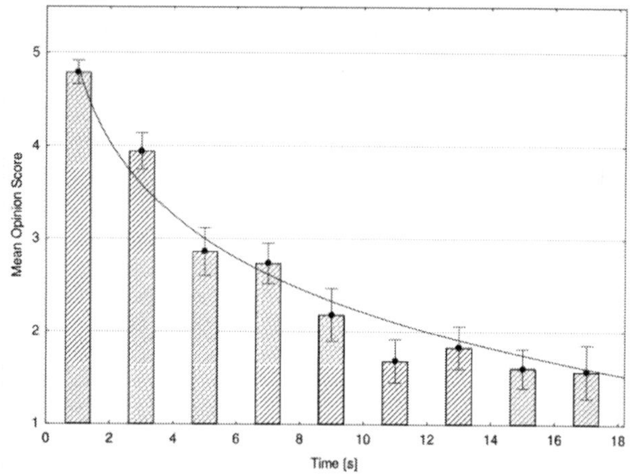

Figure 6. Page response time vs. MOS for WWW.

We made a validation of the model, using the Mann–Whitney–Wilcoxon (MWW) test [13], which showed a good estimation of the users' quality perception under the assumption of a 95% confidence interval (significance level $p<0.05$).

Similar research on the QoE model was carried out by the author for the WWW service. In this case, delay also plays a crucial role in the service delivery process [14]. There were 70 users taking part in the test and more than 1500 test measurements were conducted. Network transmission delays were controlled by a special emulator in the laboratory test-bed, where group of testers tried to use the WWW service. Two static web pages were launched on the test server and the contents of these pages were different. One of them was prepared according to ETSI reference page requirements [15] while the second was a photo gallery. The time that elapsed between the initiation of the call-up and the actual appearance of the page on the screen was measured and stored into the database. End users appraised quality subjectively (QoE) and expressed their experience in the MOS scale. The results showed that people taking part in the evaluation test were quite critical with regards to the service under analysis. A rapid decrease in the quality was observed for the web page opening times covered in the first few seconds. The longer web opening times are, the lower the grade users give, and for longer delays, especially exceeding 10 s, users' grades tend to be lower but more stable.

The obtained relation between objectively measured page response times and subjective users' grades (in the MOS scale) is presented in Figure 6. Thorough analysis of the WWW service quality as a function of the page opening time (for longer times) indicates logarithmic relationship between these values, as follows:

$$MOS = -2.6 \log_{10} T + 4.8 \qquad (2)$$

where T – web page opening time.

The models presented by (1) and (2) are valid for the emulated times between 1 s and 30 s.

For the times shorter than 1 s, the MOS value is 5. The author did not take into account the times longer than 30 s. These values were unacceptable for both the interactive messaging communication and WWW service.

The logarithmic line in Figure 6 represents the MOS value as a function of web opening times with 80 % correlation.

Statistical analysis proved that the model fits the data very well, with coefficient of determination (R2) above 0,9. It means that obtained outcomes are replicated by the model at a level of at least 90%. Confirmation of such user quality of experience distribution can be found in the analysis results presented by ITU-T in Rec. G.1030 [14].

Based on these two examples, it cannot only be seen that objective parameters describing the quality of service are important, but subjective as well. It concerns all services offered by SPs. Moreover, taking into account the users' perspective during the quality assessment process is also valuable from a business point of view. For example, for customers who want to watch a You Tube video, information regarding the number of stallings will be more important than, among others, the downlink data rate and latency.

V. Conclusion and Future Work

Many scientific papers show the relationship between QoS and QoE using metrics based on the average values of measured parameters (e.g., mean throughput, mean Round-Trip Time, etc.). It makes QoE models easier to define and understand. However, such an approach has some limitations, because it assumes that QoE is determined by the averaged stimulus.

More detailed analysis shows that transient behavior has a more significant influence on a user's perception than average values [16][17][18][19][20]. This conclusion was derived from the results of research on the quality of the WWW service, where the authors examined the influence of network bandwidth on the quality perceived by users during a Web browsing session [17].

Two scenarios were analysed: first - with a constant, and second - with a variable bandwidth. The average bandwidth in the second scenario had the same value as the constant bandwidth of the previous one (i.e., 2 Mbps). In spite of this, a significant difference in the quality experienced by the users was noted.

The QoE value, expressed in a the MOS scale, in the first case was around 4, while in the second case it dropped to 3. The characteristics of network performance, presented in some papers, indicates that taking into account the variability of transmission parameters, e.g., duration and intensity of throughput drops, leads to better QoE prediction than models based only on average throughput [21]. Another problem is how to identify a proper set of KPIs, which in turn should be measured and controlled in order to derive more precise QoE models. Currently, many of these models take into account the small number of parameters that influence the quality of services. Further work will be devoted to broadening the list of parameters that may influence the experience of users, which will help us to build more precise QoE models.

ACKNOWLEDGMENT

The author would like to thank Pawel Bardowski for his contribution to the test-bed set-up and to Zbigniew Sałamacha for his help during the editorial process.

REFERENCES

[1] ISO. *ISO 8402: Quality Management and Quality Assurance – Vocabulary*, 1994.

[2] ITU-T. *Rec. E.800: Quality of telecommunication services: concepts, models, objectives and dependability planning – Terms and definitions related to the quality of telecommunication services. Definitions of terms related to quality of service*, Geneva/Switzerland, 09/2008. [Online]. Available from: http://www.itu.int/itu-t/recommendations/rec.aspx?rec=9524, [retrieved: 12, 2017].

[3] ITU-T. *Rec. G.1000: Quality of service and performance. Communications quality of service: A framework and definitions*, Geneva/Switzerland 11/2001. [Online]. Available from: http://www.itu.int/itu-t/recommendations/rec.aspx?rec=5597, [retrieved: 12, 2017].

[4] ETSI. *ETR003: Network Aspects. General aspects of Quality of Service (QoS) and Network Performance (NP)*, 1994. [Online]. Available from: www.etsi.org, [retrieved: 12, 2017].

[5] W. C. Hardy, QoS Measurement and Evaluation of Telecommunications Quality of Service, Wiley, 2001.

[6] J. Gozdecki, A. Jajszczyk, and Rafał Stankiewicz, "Quality of Service Terminology in IP Networks," IEEE Communications Magazine, March 2003, pp. 153-159.

[7] A. Sackl and R. Schatz, "Evaluating the impact of expectations on end-user quality perception," in Proceedings of International Workshop Perceptual Quality of Systems (PQS), pp. 122–128, Vienna, Sep. 2013.

[8] E. Liotou, et al., "Shaping QoE in the 5G Ecosystem," 2015 Seventh International Workshop on Quality of Multimedia Experience (QoMEX), Greece, 2015, pp. 1-6. DOI: 10.1109/QoMEX.2015.7148089.

[9] J. Monserrat, et al., "Metis research advances towards the 5G mobile and wireless system definition," EURASIP Journal on Wireless Communications and Networking, vol. 2015, no. 1, p. 53, Mar. 2015.

[10] R. Schatz, T. Hoßfeld, L. Janowski, and S. Egger, "From packets to people: Quality of Experience as a new measurement challenge," in Data Traffic Monitoring and Analysis, ser. Lecture Notes in Computer Science, Springer Berlin Heidelberg, vol. 7754, pp. 219–263, 2013.

[11] Enders Analysis/TNS RI-Survey, May 2014.

[12] J. Klink and P. Bardowski, "Subjective quality measurements of SMS", in 22nd International Conference on Software Telecommunications & Computer Networks SoftCOM 2014, pp. 1-6, Split, Croatia, September 2014.

[13] M. P. Fay and M. A. Proschan, "Wilcoxon–Mann–Whitney or t-test? On assumptions for hypothesis tests and multiple interpretations of decision rules," Statistics Surveys 4: pp. 1–39, 2010. DOI:10.1214/09-SS051.

[14] ITU-T. *G.1030: Quality of service and performance – Generic and user-related Aspects. Estimating end-to-end performance in IP networks for data applications*, Geneva/Switzerland, 11/2005. [Online]. Available from: http://www.itu.int/itu-t/recommendations/rec.aspx?rec=12122, [retrieved: 12, 2017].

[15] ETSI. *ETSI reference page requirements*. [Online]. Available: http ://docbox.etsi.org/STQ/Open/Kepler, [retrieved: 12, 2017].

[16] A. Sackl, S. Egger, and R. Schatz, "The influence of network quality fluctuations on web QoE", in International Workshop on Quality of Multimedia Experience (IEEE QoMEX), Singapore, Sept. 2014, pp. 123-128.

[17] P. Casas, et al., "On the quest for new KPIs in mobile networks: The impact of throughput-fluctuations on QoE," in IEEE ICC 2015 - Workshop on Quality of Experience-based Management for Future Internet Applications and Services (QoE-FI), London, June 2015, pp. 1705-1710.

[18] K. Lee, J. Park, S. Lee, and A. Bovik, "Temporal Pooling of Video Quality Estimates using Perceptual Motion Models," in IEEE ICIP, 2010, pp. 2493-2496.

[19] B. Lewcio, B. Belmudez, A. Mehmood, M. Wältermann, and S. Möller, "Video Quality in Next Generation Mobile Networks – Perception of Time-Varying Transmission," in IEEE CQR, 2011, pp. 1-6.

[20] M. Seufert, M. Slanina, S. Egger, and M. Kottkamp, "To Pool or not to Pool: A Comparison of Temporal Pooling Methods for HTTP Adaptive Video Streaming," in QoMEX, 2013, pp. 52-57.

[21] A. Sackl, P. Casas, R. Schatz, L. Janowski, and R Irmer, "Quantifying the impact of network bandwidth fluctuations and outages on web QoE," in International Workshop on Quality of Multimedia Experience (IEEE QoMEX), Greece, May 2015, pp. 1-6.

[22] L. Pierucci, "The Quality of Experience Perspective Toward 5G Technology," IEEE Wireless Communications, August 2015, pp. 10-16.

QoE and QoS by Triple Play Services: A Comparison Study

Tadeus Uhl
Maritime University of Szczecin
Szczecin, Poland
email: t.uhl@am.szczecin.pl

Paweł Bardowski
Wrocław University of Science and Technology
Wrocław, Poland
email: pawel.bardowski@pwr.edu.pl

Abstract— **The applications available on the Internet can generally be divided into three categories: audio, video and data. This has given rise to the popular term Triple Play Services. Quality of Service is currently especially important in digital networks and can now be measured in two ways: subjective techniques and objective techniques. This paper elaborates on the most important techniques for measuring Quality of Experience (QoE) and Quality of Service (QoS) in Triple Play Services, comparing the most widely used QoE and QoS measurement methods in several series of analyses.**

Keywords-Triple Play Service; QoS; QoE; VoIP; VSoIP; WWW.

I. INTRODUCTION

In modern digital networks, it is not difficult to identify three parties: network providers, service providers, and users. All three parties have a common interest: Quality of Service (QoS). When the quality of service in networks is there, everybody is happy. In order to be sure that quality of service is being delivered, QoS measurements must be constantly made, and should the quality of service fall for any reason, countermeasures must be taken immediately. Preventive measures are, of course, preferable to corrective measures, and monitoring is best done unobtrusively in the background and fully automatically (cf. Figure 1).

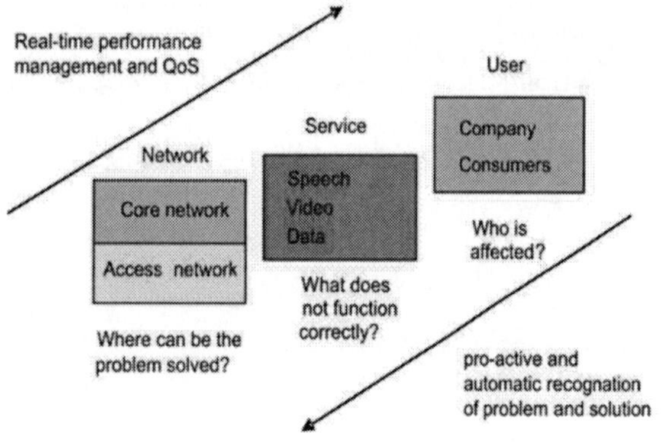

Figure 1. The three parties in digital networks.

In order to determine the QoS/QoE in a network, two models are generally used: a) the dual-ended model and b) the single-ended model [1]. In the case of the dual-ended model, two signals are used: a) the original signal and b) the degraded signal. These two signals are available uncompressed. For this reason, measurements can be carried out for both Quality of Experience (QoE, a subjective evaluation) and Quality of Service (QoS, an objective evaluation). In the case of the single-ended model, only the impaired signal (compressed) is available. This allows normally only an objective evaluation of QoS to be made (exception ITU-T P.563 [2]).

Two measurement techniques can be used in the two models cited: a) signal-based and b) parameter-based measurement. The dual-ended model uses specialised algorithms to compare the input and output signals of signal-based measurements. In the case of the single-ended model this comparison is not possible. In this case, the QoS will be determined by using the degraded signal only. In both cases, the system to be assessed is treated as a "black box". When carrying out parameter-based measurements, a distinction is made between two types: a) "glass-box" and b) "black-box". In the first case, both the structure of the system to be assessed and the reaction of the individual system components to the reference signal are known. This knowledge is then taken into consideration in a suitable model. Additionally, the network parameters measured can be included in the calculation of the QoS. In the second case, not all details of the system to be assessed are known, so only the measured network parameters and the characteristic parameters for the respective service are taken into account.

QoE refers to the appraisal of quality by test persons—the end users. It is an extremely complicated method: among other things it relies on reference signals that have been specially recorded in sound and video studios. The room, too, in which the audio and video tests are conducted, must also be specially designed. Even the selection of the test persons proves to be problematic. To achieve any reliable results at all series upon series of tests must be run. This understandably takes a lot of time and involves a lot of specialised equipment. The method is therefore fully unsuitable for analyses of quality in real networks. That is why great efforts have been made to simulate the human eye and the human ear with electronic means and to incorporate those simulations in QoE algorithms.

QoS works on the principle of parametrised models. Naturally, test persons had to be involved during the development stage of the models, which was costly, time-consuming and elaborate. Once developed, however, QoS models can be used quickly and without the need for test persons in real environments to evaluate all manner of electronic service. This is the great benefit of using parametrised QoS models and the reason why they were developed.

This paper will review and discuss the application of common QoE/QoS measuring methods to Triple Play Services (audio/video/data).

In Section II, the QoE/QoS in the VoIP service (audio) will be described. Section III provides information about QoE/QoS in the VSoIP service (video). Following that, Section IV discusses QoE/QoS in the WWW service (data). The paper concludes with a summary and an outlook on future work.

II. QoE and QoS in the VoIP Service

The most widely used QoE measurement techniques for the VoIP service are currently PESQ [3] and POLQA [4]. Both techniques are very accurate; they are, however, time-consuming and can often only be implemented with a licence. Both algorithms incorporate an electronic emulation of the human ear, so it is permissible here to speak of QoE values.

The most widely used QoS measurement techniques for the VoIP service are currently the E Model [5] and E(IP) Model [6]. Both of them are parametrised models. They are very practical: easy to use and time-saving. They do not need reference signals, which is a great benefit in practice. But how good are parametrised models in comparison with QoE measurement techniques?

To answer this question several analyses were conducted during the course of the work presented in this paper, using the numerical tool QoSCalc(VoIP) [7] (see there also the setting parameters for investigations). Figure 2 shows some quite representative results.

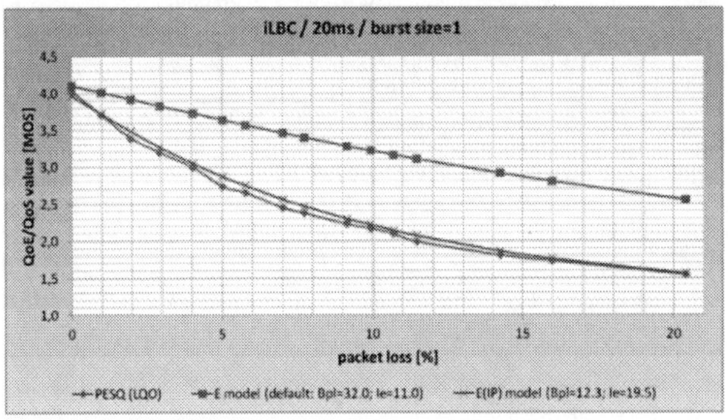

Figure 2. QoE/QoS values as a function of packet loss for different measurement techniques (codec iLBC).

It is evident that the curves from the PESQ algorithm and the E(IP) Model agree whilst the curve for the E Model deviates significantly. The E Model is unsuitable for analyses in an IP environment. The study has confirmed that with a suitable parametrised QoS model values can be achieved that come very close to QoE values. This is of substantial practical benefit!

III. QoE and QoS in the VSoIP Service

The most widely used QoE measurement techniques for the VSoIP service are currently PEVQ (J.247) [8] and VQuad-HD (J.341) [9]. These techniques are very accurate; they are, however, time-consuming and can often only be implemented with a licence. Both algorithms incorporate an electronic emulation of the human eye and so one can justifiably speak of QoE values.

The most widely used QoS measurement techniques for the VSoIP service are currently Rec. ETSI 101 290 [10] and the VSoIP Model [11]. Both measurement techniques are classed as parametrised models because they work on the basis of network and service parameters. In practice, they are quick and easy to use. They need no reference signal, which is of great practical value. But how good are parametrised models in comparison with QoE measurement techniques?

To answer this question several analyses were conducted during the course of the work described in this paper, using the numerical tool QoSCalc(IPTV) [12] (see there also the setting parameters for investigations). Figure 3 presents some typical results.

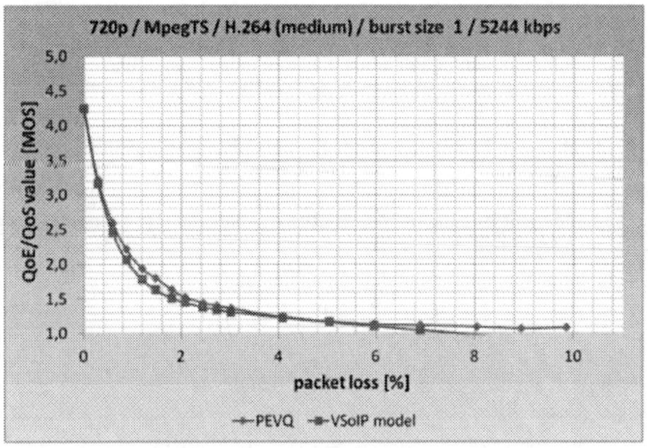

Figure 3. QoE/QoS values as a function of packet loss for different measurement techniques (codec H.264/720p).

It is evident that the curves for the PEVQ algorithm and for the VSoIP Model concur. This demonstrates unequivocally that by using a suitable parametrised QoS model it is possible to achieve values that come very close to QoE values. Another great practical benefit for all involved!

IV. QoS/QoE in the WWW Service

At present there is only one standardised technique for measuring QoE in the WWW service: Rec. ITU-T G.1030 [13]. This method requires the participation of test persons and takes only one criterion into consideration: the web page opening time, which is actually of little practical significance.

The widely used QoS measurement techniques for the WWW service are currently Apdex Index [14] and Power Metric [15]. But they have not been standardised, meaning that there is an enormous need for further developments in this area, especially in view of the fact that the WWW service is one of the most widely used applications in the Internet and accounts for the lion's share of traffic. Here, too, the question arises: Just how good are the parametrised models in comparison with QoE measurement techniques?

In order to answer this question, some results from analysis [16] (see there also the setting parameters for investigations) are presented here. Figure 4 shows quite typical results that were gained (black dots indicate the mean values, the rectangles the standard deviation).

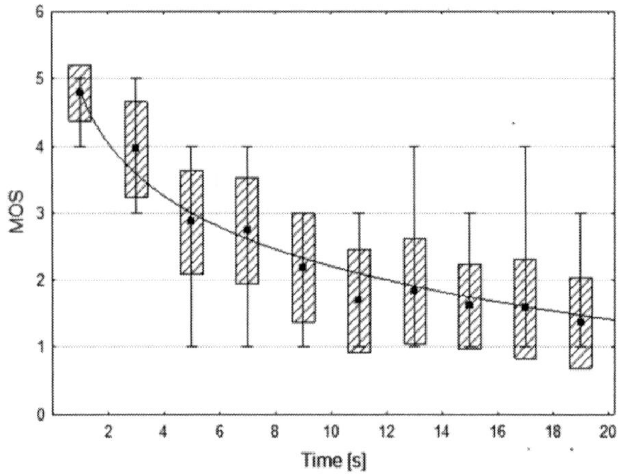

Figure 4. QoE values as a function of web page opening time for the service WWW.

It is evident that the QoE curve is subject to a logarithmic function [15]:

$$QoS_{MOS} = 4.84 - 2.63 \cdot \log T \qquad (1)$$

where T is the web page opening time.

The parametrised QoS model (given in (1)) is so simple because it is contains only one system variable: web page opening time. In order to take further system variables into consideration, the metric called Power [14] must be used. It has been demonstrated yet again that a parametrised QoS model is quick and easy to use. This is of great practical benefit!

V. Conclusion and Future Work

This paper has reviewed and discussed briefly the application of common QoE/QoS measuring methods in Triple Play Services (audio/video/data). The strengths and weaknesses of the individual QoS/QoE measurement techniques have been spelt out. It has been shown that by using suitable parametrised QoS models values can be achieved that come very close to QoE values. In practice it is highly beneficial to work with parameterised QoS models.

The number of electronic services in the Internet is increasing steadily. The philosophy behind the networks has changed: whereas networks have had clearly defined properties until recently, they are now assuming new properties dynamically during live operation. What effects will this have on the Quality of Service? Should we perhaps in future speak of Quality of Live (QoL) instead of Quality of Service (QoS)? It is a development in networks that must be followed at all costs. The authors are already planning future work in this direction.

References

[1] T. Uhl, "Quality of Service Everywhere". Proceedings of the 9th International Conferences on Advanced Service Computing, Athens/Greece, February 2017, ISBN 978-1-61208-528-9, pp. 28-30.

[2] ITU-T. *Standard ITU-T P.563: Single-ended method for objective speech quality assessment in narrow-band telephony applications.* [Online]. Available from: http://www.itu.int/rec/T-REC-P.563/en/2018.01.10.

[3] ITU-T. *Standard ITU-T P.862: PESQ.* [Online]. Available from: http://www.itu.int/rec/T-REC-P.862/en/2018.01.10.

[4] ITU-T. *Standard ITU-T P.863: POLQA.* [Online]. Available from: http://www.itu.int/rec/T-REC-P.863/en/2018.01.10.

[5] ITU-T. *Standard ITU-T G.107: E Model.* [Online]. Available from: http://www.itu.int/rec/T-REC-G.107/en/2018.01.10.

[6] German Patent and Trade Mark Office. *E(IP) model,* German Patent no. 102010044727, September 2014.

[7] S. Paulsen and T. Uhl, " Numerical tool for the investigation of the QoS in VoIP". Proceedings of the GI/ITG Workshops MMBnet'13, Hamburg/Germany, 5-6 September 2013, pp. 85-90.

[8] ITU-T. *Standard ITU-T J.247: Objective perceptual multimedia video quality measurement in the presence of a full reference.* [Online]. Available from: http://www.itu.int/rec/T-REC-J.247-200808-I/2018.01.10.

[9] ITU-T. *Standard ITU-T J.341: Objective perceptual multimedia video quality measurement of HDTV for digital cable television in the presence of a full reference.* [Online]. Available from: http://www.itu.int/rec/T-REC-J.341-201101-I/en/2018.01.10.

[10] ETSI *Rec. ETSI 101 290.* [Online]. Available from: http://www.itu.int/rec/T-REC-J.341-201101-I/en/2018.01.10.

[11] German Patent and Trade Mark Office. *VSoIP Model,* German Patent Application no. 102016207785, July 2017.

[12] T. Uhl and H. Jürgensen, "New Tool for Examining QoS in the IPTV Service". Proceedings of the WTC'14 (World Telecommunications Congress), Berlin/Germany, 1-3 June 2014.

[13] ITU-T. *Standard ITU-T G.1030: Estimating end-to-end performance in IP networks for data applications.* [Online]. Available from: http://www.itu.int/rec/T-REC-G.1030/en/2018.01.10.

[14] Apdex Alliance. *Application Performance Index - Apdex Technical Specification Version 1.1.* [Online]. Available from: http://www.apdex.org/specs.html/2018.01.10.

[15] T. Uhl, J. Klink and P. Bardowski, "New metric for World Wide Web Service Quality", Journal of Telecommunication and Information Technology, no. 2, pp. 50–58, June 2014.

[16] J. Klink, "A new approach to WWW service quality evaluation". Proceedings of the 22nd Conference on Software, Telecommunications and Computer Networks (SoftCOM), Split/Croatia, Sept. 17-19, 2014.

The Impact of Cyber Security on the Quality of Service in Optical Networks

Michal Walkowski, Jacek Oko, Slawomir Sujecki
Department of Telecommunications and Teleinformatics
Wroclaw University of Science and Technology,
Wroclaw, Poland
Emails: michal.walkowski@pwr.edu.pl.
jacek.oko@pwr.edu.pl
slawomir.sujecki@pwr.edu.pl

Stanislaw Kozdrowski
Department of Telecommunications and Teleinformatics
Wroclaw University of Science and Technology,
Wroclaw, Poland
Email: s.kozdrowski@tele.pw.edu.pl

***Abstract*— We analyze the impact of novel solutions for cloud computing implementation on the operation of an optical network in the context of cloud computing structures applied within a large corporation networking environment. We focus particularly on various aspects of the quality of service that are related to an implementation of a particular solution to an improvement of various aspects of cyber security. We present the methods of improving the cyber security, the quality of service and compare them with those currently in use.**

Keywords-cloud-computing; network; containcers, security, qualyty of service.

I. INTRODUCTION

With an increase in the data flow volume, we observe an introduction of ever newer technologies needed to support the network traffic. In recent years the dominant technology for the handling of large data throughput is based on the use of optical fibers. The maximum currently achievable data transmission rates have been achieved in Wavelength Division Multiplexed (WDM) systems and hence WDM, is the key technology used now for the realization of the backbone networks [1][2]. Also, large data transmission rates in access networks are realized using optical fiber technology. Obviously, new technological solutions need to be accompanied by new solutions in the higher layers of the OSI model in order to insure the quality of service. Also a careful analysis of potential weaknesses of new technology with respect to cyber security is needed and potentially new solutions are required to handle all potential threats [3]. All this poses new challenges to the quality of service in modern telecom networks. The general purpose of this research is an analysis of the impact of various cyber security measures on the operation of an optical network in the context of cloud computing structures applied within a large corporation networking environment. We focus particularly on various aspects of the quality of service that are related to an implementation of a particular solution to an improvement of various aspects of cyber security. We present the discussion in the context of several possible attack scenarios and draw conclusions on this basis. In particular, we consider the cyber security solutions that are implemented in the optical layer and discuss also the cost and network maintenance implications of such solutions. We present the methods of improving the cyber security within the optical layer and compare them with those potentially applicable in the higher layers of the OSI model. We stress particularly the impact of the various measures on the quality of service but also discuss the issues related to the cost and network maintenance. A specific issue that we address in this contribution is a specific new solution in the area of the cloud computing recently being pursued in the context of the ever increasing data transmission rates and cyber security requirements, which relies on the implementation of Docker containerization. This solution is particularly attractive for an implementation in large scale enterprise network systems.

II. LARGE SCALE ENTERPRISE NETWORK SYSTEMS

Large scale enterprise (LSE) network systems serve both the employees of the enterprise and the external customers. Such networks can spread over large geographical areas thus implying large distances between the network nodes.

A new trend of development in the large scale enterprise networks introduces concept of micro-services. The concept of micro-services means that each single service should provide only one solution for a particular problem as well as be stateless and independent at the same time. For the purpose of solving the requirements set by programmers, technology of Docker containerization has been created. The main difference when compared with the so far used virtual machine solution (Figure 1) [4] is that container does not need to run operating system stack for a new service. Additionally, it allows to run the same application without customizing the operating system on each side. This results in lesser overhead when delivering service to customer. The programmer gets exactly the same environment as the client, so potential problems with providing services should be this minimized.

In the industrial research context there are two important orchestrators for managing Docker ecosystem, Swarm and Kompose. The second one is provided by OpenShift software developed by RedHat (RHEL) (Figure 3) [5]. Software supporting both solutions is currently available on

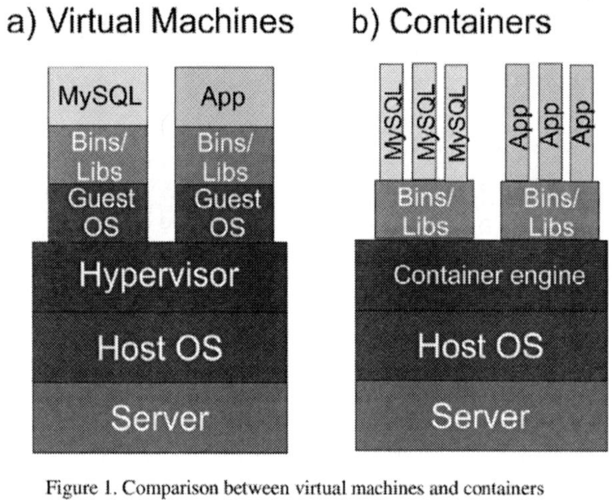

Figure 1. Comparison between virtual machines and containers

the internet and has already been implemented in many institutions (LSE) working on critical services from end users' point of view.

Technology consists of cloud computing, which is based on communication between machines serving services, divided into roles (master, node, load balancer, present master state storage, data storage). Currently the software supporting the Docker system allows achieving for one cluster up to 2 000 nodes and 120 000 containers.

III. SERVICE QUALITY

Container technology allows to measure and monitor services health (e.g., user CPU, system CPU usage) and thus provides for implementation of automatic vertical scaling when system is overloaded. This helps improving the service quality. Internal load balancer can successively control the external traffic coming from the clients of the network (Figure 2). When more capabilities are needed, usage of other software or hardware tools is possible. For instance we can implement an in-house developed balancer.

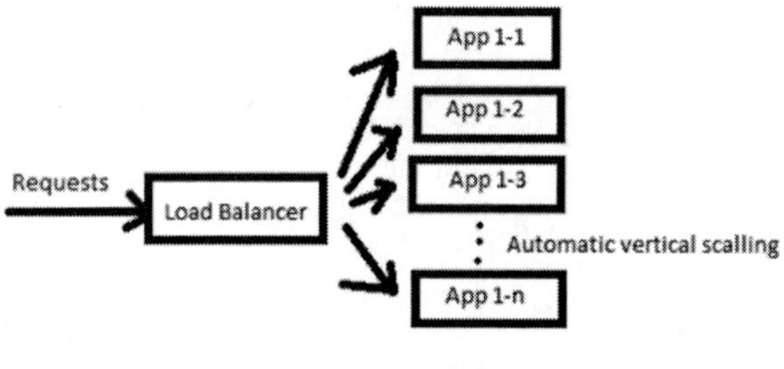

Figure 2. Load Balancer with automatic scaling

An additional advantage is that the Docker system can detect problem with internal network, cluster or machine and respond appropriately, preserving this way high Disaster Recovery (DR) and High Availability (HA) (Figure 4). If vertical scaling is not sufficient, system administrator can add new nodes to the existing infrastructure. The related research is carried out at several laboratories, e.g., [5] and aims to

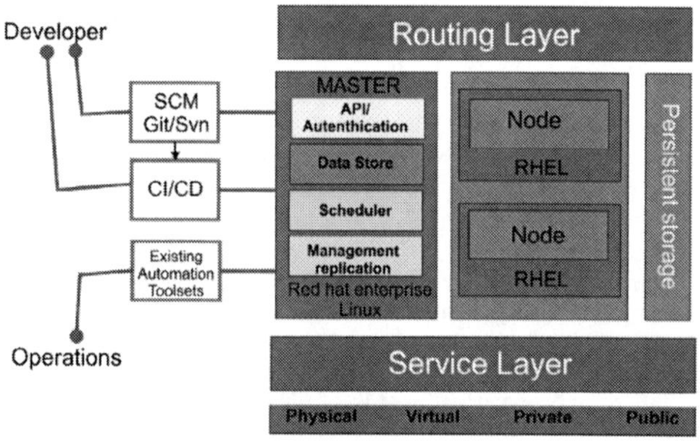

Figure 3. Architecture of OpenShift

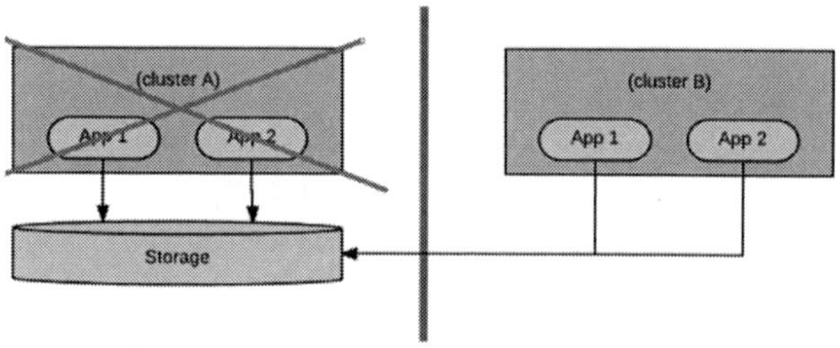

Figure 4. High availability mechanism

improve internal communication between the containers. Particular attention is devoted to the development of algorithms, which introduce priority for containers that speed up information exchange [6].

IV. POSSIBILE ATTACKS

Next, we consider the problem of insuring cyber-security within a Docker ecosystem. Firstly, we need to identify possible threats. There are several ways in which a cyber-attack can be performed on a Docker based system. Firstly we note that by default all Docker containers share the same network. Therefore, a specially prepared container can use Address Resolution Protocol (ARP) poisoning to disrupt or capture communication between services, thus essentially to perform potentially a man in the middle attack. Another problem concerning cyber-security is that in a Docker system the daemon is able to use an administrator's rights for proper operations. In this scenario an attacker can potentially escape from the container context and even attempt to overtake the control of all the system nodes.

The third possible threat emerges when Docker images are downloaded from untrusted sources, which results in risks of information leakage or botnet creation [7].

There is also a problem with identifying the container, which was attacked. For instance, if hypervisor host OS is not fully proof to an attack, a container can be successfully attacked without the possibility for carrying out a comprehensive forensic analysis because an attacker can remove all the traces of the attack. This is because when a container is created it has its own ID rather than IP address. Hence, from outside IP addresses are the same for more than one container. Containers are created and send log to the SIEM in LSE so after creating more the one container we cannot track them using an IP address. Consequently, we cannot do comprehensive forensics because we are not able to identify the container which was attacked.

V. Protection Mechanisms

The possible attack scenarios described in the previous section can be mitigated in several ways. First of all, it is worth to mention Center for Information Security (CIS) Security Benchmark documentation, which provides conditions needed to secure Docker configuration. This document gives general guidelines on how a Docker system security can be improved.

In this contribution, we propose and give special attention to the following methods/guidelines of improving cyber-security within a Docker system:

- application inside the container should not be run with an administrator rights
- each system component should log to system of logs correlation e.g. Security Information and Event Monitoring (SIEM)
- good practice is to run only one process inside the container.
- all of the libraries needed in development time and not needed anymore in the production should be removed
- running services for remote application configuration inside container is prohibited, e.g. ssh, telnet
- hardcoring keys, passwords and other sensitive data needed for communication or encryption is prohibited

We note however that all of the methods outlined above can only make it harder for an attacker to get into the system but they do not provide total security. In the future, we will continue research on how these measures improve the system stability and security and how they impact on the quality of service.

VI. Conclusion and Future Work

In the era of progressing computerization, the threat to IT systems is increasing. The paper discusses the security and service quality issues within a large scale enterprise network based on cloud computing which uses the Docker system. This discussion shows that there is a real need to control and monitor possible threats, which prompts further research into this field.

Thus our future work will be focused on the development and implementation of an elastic solution for improving security in corporate networks based on cloud computing. Our main aim is to develop algorithms that will process the data compiled from the vulnerability and compliance scanners e.g., Qualys, Nessus or Inspect, in an optimal way. The algorithm should also provide useful information about the security level in the corporate assets (Figure 5). Further, the developed algorithm should be scalable to handle efficiently increasing amounts of data. Finally, the algorithm should communicate with the Docker orchestrator to dynamically respond to an increased demand by allocating more resources from the cloud server.

Figure 5. Architecture of proposed system

Acknowledgment

The authors wish to thank anonymous reviewers for valuable comments and remarks and Wrocław University of Science and Technology (statutory activity) for financial support.

REFERENCES

[1] Y. Li, L. Gao, G. Shen, and L. Peng, "Impact of ROADM Colorless, Directionless, and Contentionless (CDC) Features on Optical Network", J. Opt. Commun. Netw. B58-B67, 2012.

[2] T. Zami, "Multiflow Application for WDM Networks With Multicarrier Transponders Serving Superchannels in Contentionless OXCs", J. Opt. Commun. Netw. A114-A124, 2017.

[3] K. Hashizume, D. G. Rosado, E Fernandez-Medina, and E. B. Fernandez, "An analysis of securit issues for cloud computing", Journal of Internet Serices And Applications, London , 2013.

[4] URL:https://qafe.com/what-is-docker-why-en-how-use-it/ [accessed: 15.12.201].

[5] URL:https://docs.openshift.com/container-platform/3.7/architecture/index.html, [accessed: 15.12.2017].

[6] A. Dusia, Y. Yang, and M. Taufer, "Network Quality of Service in Docker Containers", IEEE Conference on Cluster Computing, Chicago, USA, 2015.

[7] T. Bui, "Analysis of Docker Security", Aalto University, Helsinki, Finland, 2015

Optical Node Architectures in the Context of the Quality of Service in Optical Networks

Stanisław Kozdrowski

Institute of Telecommunications,
Warsaw University of Technology
Warsaw, Poland
Email: s.kozdrowski@tele.pw.edu.pl

Sławomir Sujecki

Department of Telecommunications and Informatics,
Wrocław University of Science and Technology
Wrocław, Poland
Email: slawomir.sujecki@pwr.edu.pl

***Abstract*—We show a new generation reconfigurable add drop optical node architecture in the context of evolution of the flexible photonic layer in telco networks. We compare the proposed node architecture with the existing classic reconfigurable optical add drop multiplexer (ROADM) architectures and also directionless, colorless and gridless techniques. We focus particularly on various aspects of the quality of service in optical network, such as blocking probability and full automation including touchless provisioning of bandwidth and a reduction of manual errors. Additionally, we stress the benefits of the proposed node architecture in both near term and long term future.**

***Keywords*–DWDM network; node architecture; reconfigurable optical add/drop; CDC optical node; QoS; blocking probability.**

I. Introduction

Optical networks are undergoing significant changes due to the exponential growth of traffic (e.g., internet traffic, increasing demands for multimedia and cloud computing). The continuous growth of customer IP traffic in combination with high-rate applications, such as video on demand, high definition TV, cloud computing and data center storage systems require cost-effective and scalable networking infrastructure. It is predicted that IP traffic will grow still rapidly in the next years [1]. This prompts for increasing the capacity and transport efficiency of optical networks in order to realize all client demands and to be able to guarantee high Quality of Service (QoS) that is crucial within a large corporation networking environment (i.e., financial corporation, banks, network providers). On the other hand, the design of a modern optical network has to have an ability to accommodate both large demands (e.g., 1Tb) and a small ones (e.g. 1 Gb). For example, multi-core processing network storage or cloud computing applications are requesting data flows from 1 Gb up to 1 Tb. Existing Dense Wavelength Division Multiplexing (DWDM) network operators provide 10 Gb, 100 Gb, 400 Gb and 1 Tb bit rates and therefore a flexible node architecture is needed.

In recent years, the reconfigurable optical add/drop multiplexers (ROADMs) have been widely deployed in DWDM networks [2]. ROADM enables in a flexible way to add and drop WDM channels without manual engineer intervention at the network operator site [3][4]. However, most current network operators have still ROADM nodes with limited automatic provisioning. ROADM architectures for colourless, directionless and contentionless (CDC) WDM nodes are of great interest for future generation optical networks since they allow access to any colour and arbitrary direction from any transponder within a network node [5]. Such architectures enhance network flexibility and increase QoS. Also they improve overall availability and simplify routing algorithms for network management. The deployment of advanced CDC ROADMs node architectures and implementation of generalized multiprotocol label switching (GMPLS) within control plane in DWDM networks are another significant advantages. Such activity causes the close cooperation among vendors and network operators [6]. It is currently one of the major drivers for network operators to deploy GMPLS in their DWDM networks, mainly because of failure survivability and very quick network restoration after a failure event. This significantly increases QoS of optical networks from the network customer point of view.

Flexible grid spectrum is another important feature of modern WDM networks and is a way for operators to future-proof networks that will ultimately need to content with transport speed beyond 100 Gb/s bit rate [7]. The proposed solution is a more granular version of the ITU grid that brakes spectrum down to 6.25 GHz granularities [8]. Low utilization in provisioning a lightpath becomes more severe when the frequency slot granularity becomes larger. For example, it is spectrally efficient for an optical channel with 12.5 GHz frequency spacing to carry a 40 Gb/s lightpath. However, it will be spectrally wasteful for the same lightpath if 25 GHz frequency spacing is applied. From this perspective, for better spectrum utilization a gridless allocation mode was evaluated [9].

One of the most profound engineering problems in optical network is refered to as the Routing and Spectrum Allocation (RSA) problem and essentially consists in finding currently unoccupied spectrum resources to establish a given set of lightpaths in a traffic efficient way with respect to a future demand. Due to the spectrum contiguity constraint, the RSA optimization problem is NP-hard, considerably more challenging than the corresponding Routing and Wavelength Assignment (RWA) problem in fixed-grid networks [10][11]. During the last decade the RSA problem attracted a considerable attention of the telecommunications community. In effect, numerous exact and heuristic approaches for solving various RSA instances are now available [12][13]. On the other hand, an important problem concerning optimal cost design of Elastic Optical Networks (EON) was investigated [14] - namely the problem of optimizing the configuration of sliceable-bandwidth variable transceivers (S-BVT) in the EON nodes. In our opinion, however, all those approaches have a common drawback in that, they do not effectively treat the optical node.

In this paper, we focus on the optical node architectures in optical DWDM networks. We compare them and show the benefits of such solution in the near term and long term future of optical DWDM networks.

The rest of this paper is organized as follows. In Section II, we present optical node architectures. Then, in Section III we focus on the benefits of the architectures. Last Section concludes the paper and shortly describes our future work.

II. Optical Node Architectures

New Generation Reconfigurable Optical Add Drop Multiplexers (NG ROADM) consist of four functionalitiess: directionless, colourless, contentionless and flex grid (CDC-F). The functions can be deployed all together or in different combinations, such as CD, CDC or CDC-F.

A. Conventional ROADM

Classic ROADM architectures have two important limitations. Firstly, they are coloured. This means that each transponder coresponds to a fixed wavelength. The second constraint is that the add/drop process is directional. This means that outband direction of the add signals is limited to the same degree and can not reach other ROADM degree. This prevents the added signals to be routed to different optical paths and thus limits the flexibility of the node and the network. An illustrative example of conventional ROADM is depicted in Figure 1.

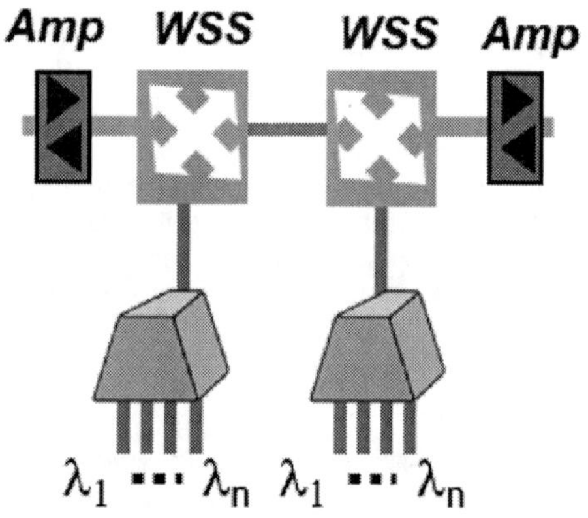

Figure 1. Conventional ROADM. Designed for metro to long haul infrastructures with mesh connectivity.

B. Directionless ROADM

The NG ROADM needs to have the directionless functionalities. It is defined that for any channel dropped at the local node, the coresponding add channel can go to any output port, regardless of which input port it comes from. The directionless feature allows more efficient sharing of transponder in a node among different ports, and therefore improves the protection process. Figure 2 shows the functional schematic of directionless feature.

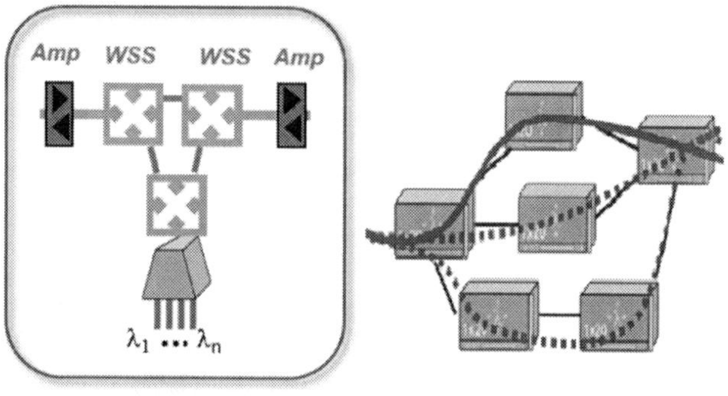

Figure 2. Directionless ROADM. Remotely route wavelenghts across any viable path.

C. Colourless ROADM

Network operators are demanding colourless functionality for NG ROADM, where the add/drop ports are not wavelength specific and any transponder can be tuned to any channel (colour). This feature allows full automation of wavelength assignment. Colorless feature also allows the network operator to use different wavelength for different sections in the optical paths to avoid congestion situation in the network. Directionless and colourless ROADMs are increasingly being discussed together as "must haves" for true optical layer flexibility.

Colorless ROADM node architectures automate the assignment of add/drop wavelength functionality. There are several variations for building colourless ROADMs. Regardless of architectures approach, the final result is that any wavelength (colour) can be assigned to any port at the add/drop site, completely by software control and tunable transponders, now widely deployed, without any technician intervention on site. An example of colourless ROADM architecture is depicted in Figure 3.

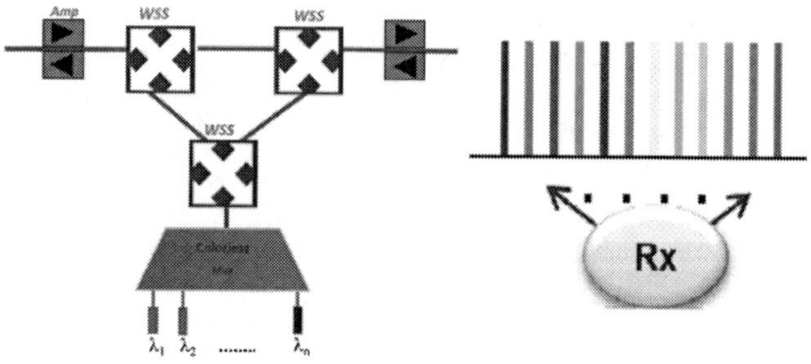

Figure 3. Colourless ROADM. Reconfigurable and restorable infrastructure. Receive any wavelength on any port.

D. Contentionless ROADM

The notions of colourless and directionless ROADMs have been discussed within the industrial research community and by optical network operators for a number of years now. The concept of contentionless ROADM networks, on the other hand, is fairly new and was introduced only relatively recently. The main driving the factor behind contentionless ROADMs is the fact that even with colourless and directionless functionality, a ROADM network still has severe limitations. Namely, in a colourless or directionless ROADM network a manual on site intervention may still be required. In other words, a colourless or directionless ROADM network is not fully flexible.

Another problem inherent to colourless and directionless ROADM networks is that a wavelength blocking event may occur when two wavelengths of the same colour arrive simultaneously at the same WSS structure, which results in wavelength contention. A network operator may avoid an occurrence of such wavelength contention events by partitioning the add/drop structure so that differently coloured wavelengths are associated with different structures. In this way the possibility of a simultaneous arrival of two identical wavelengths at the same add/drop structure is eliminated. However, it needs to be noted that whilst such solution eliminates an occurrence of wavelength contention from a channel provisioning perspective, it reduces at the same time the dynamic flexibility of the network. Further, an additional add/drop structure is required to handle the traffic when two wavelengths compete for the same WDM channel. Therefore, a more effective solution of the problem is an introduction of a contentionless ROADM architecture. The contentionless ROADM architecture, illustrated in Figure 4, by contrast, allows multiple copies of the same wavelength to be handled by a single add/drop structure.

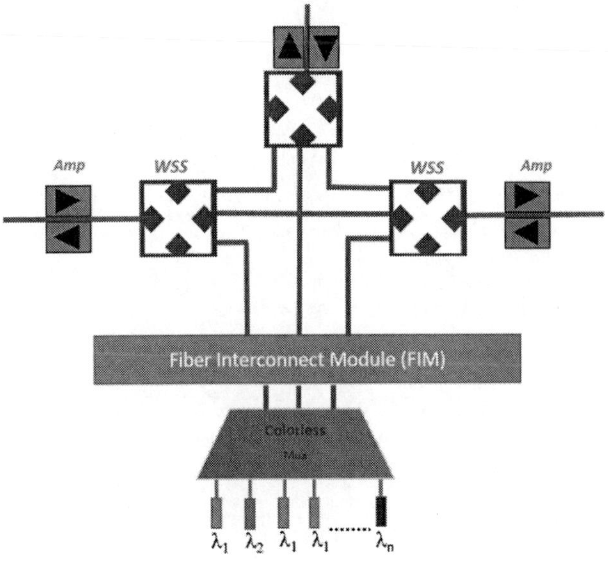

Figure 4. Contentionless ROADM is able to add and/drop the same wavelength on the same mux/demux module. In this particular 3-degree ROADM CDC architecture there is possible to add/drop 3 λ_1 (green colour) on the same mux/demux module.

Hence, a colourless/directionless architecture combined with truly contentionless functionality is the end goal from the perspective of any network operator that has deployed - or is planning to deploy - a ROADM network. Such architectures, namely colourless, directionless, contentionless (CDC), offer an ultimate level of flexibility in the optical layer.

E. Flex Spectrum

The fourth key concept in NG ROADM architectures, depicted in Figure 5, is the concept of a flexible spectrum (also called gridless WDM). The flexible spectrum is a way for operators to future-proof networks that will ultimately need to contend with transport speeds beyond 100 Gb/s. For speeds beyond 100 Gb/s - i.e., 400 Gb/s or 1 Tb/s - more than 50 GHz of spectrum may be required. Network operators would also like to be able to accommodate those future transmission speeds using the same 40 G and 100G ROADM networks.

In essence, gridless WDM is a more granular version of the ITU grid that breaks spectrum down to 6.25 GHz inter-channel spectral distance. Thus, ROADM nodes supporting a flexible grid are capable of routing any WDM channel that has a bandwidth, which is a multiple of 6.25 GHz, e.g., 25 GHz, 75 GHz, etc. It is future-proof solution that prepares optical network for any higher capacity channel that needs more than 50 GHz spectrum.

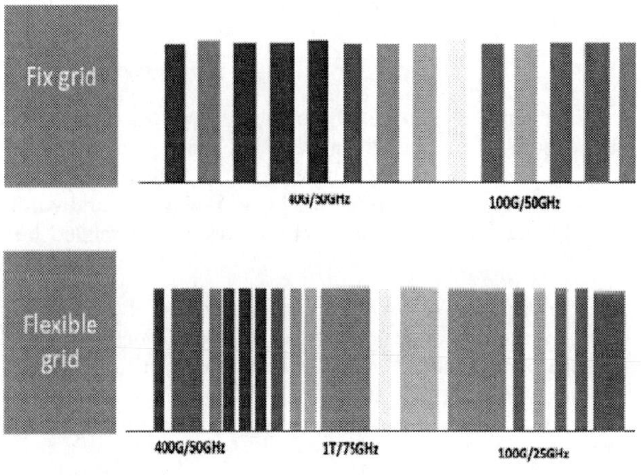

Figure 5. Fix grid and Flexible grid spectrum. Discover to increase network spectral efficiency.

III. Benefits of NG ROADM Architectures

NG ROADM architectures are of great interest to network operators since these network architectures allow connection of any wavelength from any transponder in any direction. This helps service providers to enhance network flexibility and survivability whilst reducing operational costs. Currently 100 Gb/s standard is beginning to move from long-haul networks to metro/regional networks. As operators move to metro coherent 100 Gb/s standard, they are simultaneously upgrading their layer 1 and photonic metro infrastructure. Advanced modulation schemes and super channels, enabled by coherent detection, are leading operators to future-proof their ROADM networks by deploying flex spectrum hardware today, in anticipation of variable channel widths in the future.

Another benefit is opex and capex reduction. Opex reduction is delivered primarily via the touchless provisioning and activation of network bandwidth and in particular by automating the activation of the end points of photonic layer circuits. As noted, a classic ROADM WDM system delivers a level of automation in the network by enabling touchless provisioning of bandwidth. CDC functionality eliminates the need for technician truck rolls, thus saving on labor costs as well as reduce the time to provision. Another important opex benefit delivered through automation is the reduction of manual errors and dirty connection - risks that can be completely avoided through automation.

There is also another advantage connected with the integration of NG ROADM with Optical Transport Network (OTN) solution. This solution allows network operators achieving almost optimal fiber bandwidth utilization. The gain resulting from an application of NG ROADM with OTN is significant because it provides for grooming of "smaller lambdas" (e.g., sub-wavelength level traffic like SDH, Gigabit Ethernet and Fibre Channel) and consequently the available wavelengths are utilized optimally before they are switched in the ROADM layer. Such solution leads to further capex savings by integration of OTN switches and CDC-F ROADMs within the same system. We also note that an application of a CDC-F ROADM layer allows for an implementation of Software Defined Networks (SDN) and thus allows for a multi-vendor and multi-layer integration.

IV. Conclusions and Future Work

The implementation of the flexible optical layer in backbone network optical fiber based technology is currently on the way. NG ROADM allows end to end automation and increases QoS through flexible provisioning of bandwidth, an elimination of technician visits on sites and of related human errors.

Our future work will be concentrated on the optimization of the optical node resources in optical networks and a comparison of various nodal architectures. For this purpose we intend to develop specifically tailored optimization algorithms including integer linear programing and heuristic approach.

Acknowledgment

The authors would like to thank anonymous reviewers for valuable comments and remarks, and also Wrocław University of Science and Technology (statutory activity) for financial suport.

References

[1] URL:https://www.cisco.com/c/en/us/solutions/collateral/service-provider/visual-networking-index-vni/mobile-white-paper-c11-520862.html [accessed: 2018-01-02].

[2] P. N. Ji and Y. Aono, "Colorless and directionless multi-degree reconfigurable optical add/drop multiplexers," in *Wireless and Optical Communications Conference (WOCC), 2010 19th Annual*, 11431732, (Shanghai, China), IEEE, June 2010.

[3] R. Jensen, A. Lord, and N. Parsons, "Colourless, directionless, contentionless roadm architecture using low-loss optical matrix switches," in *Optical Communication (ECOC), 2010 36th European Conference and Exhibition on Optical Communication*, (Torino, Italy), IEEE, Aug. 2010.

[4] R. Jensen, A. Lord, and N. Parsons, "Highly scalable oxc-based contentionless roadm architecture with reduced network implementation costs," *Journal of the Optical Society of America*, Mar. 2012.

[5] L. Zong, G. N. Liu, H. Zhao, T. Ma, and A. Lord, "Ultra-compact contentionless roadm architecture with high resiliance based on flexible wavelength router," *Journal of the Optical Society of America*, Aug. 2014.

[6] J. Pedro and S. Pato, "Towards fully flexible optical node architectures: Impact on blocking performance of dwdm transport networks," *ICTON*, Aug. 2011.

[7] M. Żotkiewicz, M. Ruiz, M. Pióro, and L. Velasco, "Reoptimization of dynamic flexgrid optical networks after link failure repairs," *IEEE Journal of Optical Communications and Networking*, vol. 7, pp. 49–61, Jan. 2015.

[8] W. Zheng, Y. Jin, W. Sun, W. Guo, and W. Hu, "On the spectrum-efficiency of bandwidth-variable optical ofdm transport networks," *OSA*, May 2010.

[9] G. S. Shen and Q. Yang, "From coarse grid to mini-grid to gridless: How much can gridless help contentionless?," *Journal of the Optical Society of America*, Mar. 2011.

[10] M. Klinkowski and K. Walkowiak, "Routing and spectrum assignment in spectrum sliced elastic optical path network," *IEEE Communications Letters*, vol. 15, pp. 884–886, Aug. 2011.

[11] M. Ruiz, M. Pióro, M. Żotkiewicz, M. Klinkowski, and L. Velasco, "Column generation algorithm for rsa problems in flexgrid optical networks," *Photonic Network Communications*, vol. 23, pp. 53–64, Dec. 2013.

[12] Y. Wang, X. Cao, and C. Qiao, "Minimize sub-carrier re-allocation overhead in slice networks with dynamic traffic," *Journal of the Optical Society of America*, Mar. 2013.

[13] S. Shakya and X. Cao, "Spectral defragmentation in elastic optical path networks using independent sets," *Journal of the Optical Society of America*, June 2013.

[14] A. de Sousa, A. Tomaszewski, and M. Pióro, "Bin-Packing Based Optimization of EON Networks with S-BVTs," *Optical Network Design and Modeling (ONDM), 2016 International Conference*, 2016.